5 Minute 365
DAILY
DEVOTIONAL
FOR 2-3 YEAR OLD
TODDLER
GIRLS

With Jesus and Bible Story Prayers

This book belongs to:

Table of Contents

Thank You for the little hearts that love and trust You.
May this book help us see Your goodness and grow in Your love.

Let the children come to me... for the Kingdom of heaven belongs to such as these.
(Matthew 19:14)

January

New Beginnings with God

God makes everything new!
(2 Corinthians 5:17)

Ella woke up with a big stretch and a happy giggle. "Good morning, new day!" she cheered. She ran outside, where the flowers swayed and the sun felt warm. "God makes everything new!" Mommy said. Ella twirled and clapped. Yesterday's spills and tears were gone—today was fresh and full of joy!

Just like flowers bloom again, God gives us new beginnings. When we wake up, we can smile, knowing each day is a gift. Let's dance, laugh, and enjoy God's fresh, bright world!

Reflection:

Can you show me how you would dance or clap to say "thank you" to God for a brand new day?

Today's Prayer:

Dear God, thank you for giving me a brand new day to smile and play. Please help me remember that you make everything new and fill my heart with joy.

2
JANUARY

Jesus is Your Friend
Jesus loves you and is your friend!
(John 15:15)

Isabella loves to play! One day, she found a special secret—Jesus is her friend! He loves her, just like her cuddly toy. Whether happy or sad, she talks to Him, knowing He listens and keeps her close.

Remember, Jesus loves you and is always your friend!

Reflection:

Can you show me how you would give Jesus a big hug, just like you hug your favorite toy?

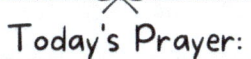

Today's Prayer:

Dear Jesus, thank you for loving me and being my special friend. Please help me feel your hugs and remember you are always with me.

3
JANUARY

Sharing and Generosity
Share what you have, and your heart will be happy! (Acts 20:35)

In a bright garden, Ellie found a basket of shiny apples. She loved them! But instead of keeping them all, she shared with her friends. "If I share, we'll all be happy!" she said. They laughed, enjoying the apples together. Sharing filled Ellie with joy! When we share, we spread love and kindness, making everyone feel special!

Reflection:
Can you show me how you would share your favorite toy or snack with a friend to make them smile?

Today's Prayer:

Dear God, thank you for giving me good things to share. Please help me be kind and make others happy by sharing with them.

4
JANUARY

Being Kind Like Jesus
Be kind to everyone, just like Jesus is kind!
(Ephesians 4:32)

Zoe loved to play! One day, she saw her friend Sadie feeling sad. Remembering Jesus' words, "Be kind to everyone," Zoe gave her a hug and shared her favorite toy. Sadie smiled, and they played happily.

Just like Zoe, we can share kindness and love. A little kindness makes a big difference—just like Jesus' love for us!

Reflection:

Can you show me a way you like to be kind to your friends, just like Zoe was kind to Sadie?

Today's Prayer:

Dear God, thank you for teaching us to be kind like Jesus. Help us to always share hugs and toys with our friends, just like Zoe did for Sadie, so we can make everyone smile.

5
JANUARY

Praying to God
You can talk to God, and He loves to listen!
(1 Thessalonians 5:17)

Have you ever talked to God? It's like having a special conversation with a friend. When you see a beautiful flower, you can say, "Thank you, God, for the pretty flower!" If you ever lose your favorite toy, you can ask God to help you find it. God loves hearing from you! Just like talking to your friends makes you happy, talking to God can make your heart feel joyful. Remember, dear child, God loves when you share your thoughts and feelings with Him!

Reflection:

Can you think of something special you want to tell God? Maybe it's a pretty flower you saw or a favorite toy you love? What would you say to Him?

Today's Prayer:

Dear God, thank you for being my best friend who loves to listen to me. Help me to talk to you every day, sharing my happy thoughts and asking for your help when I need it.

6
JANUARY

Trusting God When You're Scared
God is with you, so don't be afraid!
(Isaiah 41:10)

Once there was a brave little bunny named Beatrice. One day, Beatrice saw a big shadow and got really scared! She thought it was a giant bird, but it was just a big tree! Beatrice whispered, "God, please help me be brave." Then she took a deep breath and hopped closer. She smiled when she saw it was just the tree swaying in the wind. Beatrice learned that God was with her, even when she felt scared!

Reflection:

What do you do when you feel scared? Can you think of a time when you were scared, just like a little mouse hiding?

Today's Prayer:

Dear God, sometimes I feel scared, but I know you are always with me. Help me to trust you when I feel afraid. Thank you for loving me.

7
JANUARY

God Made You Special
You are wonderfully made!
(Psalm 139:14)

In this big, beautiful world, God made you special, just the way you are! He painted your smile and chose your giggle. Imagine a little star twinkling—just like you! Every twinkle reminds us how special we are to God. So, when you play or dance, remember, you're loved and cherished by Him!

Reflection:

Can you think of something you love about yourself that makes you special, just like the twinkling stars? What makes you smile or giggle?

Today's Prayer:

Dear God, thank you for making me special and filling my days with joy. Help me to always remember that I am loved just the way I am, just like a twinkling star in your beautiful world.

8
JANUARY

Thanking God for Everything

Thank you, God, for the sunshine and the stars! (Psalm 136:1)

Annie loves her bright land. One sunny day, she saw butterflies, flowers, and her puppy wagging its tail. "Thank you, God, for everything happy!" she sang. Are you thankful today? God loves when we say thank you for sunshine, hugs, and snacks. Every day is a joyful gift. God gives us many reasons to be thankful and joyful.

Reflection:

Can you think of something happy you saw today, like a butterfly or your puppy? Let's say thank you, God, for that special thing! What makes you smile?

Today's Prayer:

Thank you, Lord, for the beautiful butterflies, the colorful flowers, and my puppy's love. Help me to see the joyful things and remember to say thank you, just like Annie does!

9
JANUARY

Helping Others Like Jesus Did

Help others and share your toys, just like Jesus loves you! (Mark 10:16)

Friends can be like Jesus by helping others. One day, a child saw a friend fall and remembered how Jesus helped everyone. With a smile, they ran over and said, "Let me help you up!" Soon, they laughed and played together. Helping others fills our hearts with joy, just like Jesus! Whenever you see someone in need, share kindness and brighten their day.

Reflection:

When you see a friend who needs help, how do you think it makes your heart feel to help them, just like Lily helped her friend?

Today's Prayer:

Thank you for the angels who guide me in loving others and helping those in need. Please fill my heart with kindness so I can share smiles and support my friends, just like you do.

10
JANUARY

Listening to Parents and God

Listen to your mom and dad,
for they love you so! (Ephesians 6:1)

Children love to play in their cozy home. One sunny day, a parent says, "Let's pick up your toys!" They listen, knowing their parents love them and want them to be happy. With a big smile, they help tidy up, remembering that listening brings joy to God too! Let's be good listeners, showing love and respect, just like the children who listen to their mom and dad.

Reflection:

When you hear your parent say, "Let's pick up your toys!" how do you feel inside? Do you feel happy helping them? Can you think of a time when you listened and it made your home cozy and fun?

Today's Prayer:

Dear God, thank you for my family who loves me and helps me learn. Please help me listen with a happy heart and show love by helping at home.

11
JANUARY

Obeying God's Word

Do what God says! His words are good for you!
(John 14:15)

Once there was a little girl named Lily who loved to play outside. One day, mommy said, "Lily, when I call you, you need to come right away!" Lily wanted to climb the big tree, but she remembered what mommy said. So, when mommy called, Lily ran to her quickly! Mommy smiled and gave her a big hug. Lily was happy because she obeyed, and now they could play together.

Reflection:

What are some ways you can listen and follow the things God wants you to do today? Can you think of a time you listened to your parents like how we listen to God?

Today's Prayer:

Dear God, thank you for loving me and helping me to listen to you. Please help me to obey your words and make good choices. Amen.

7

12
JANUARY

Jesus' Teachings on Love
Love each other just as I love you.
(John 15:12)

Jesus shared a beautiful secret about love: "Love each other like I love you." Imagine giving hugs and sharing toys with friends— those are love hugs and love smiles! When we show kindness, we sprinkle happiness everywhere! Just like a little flower blooming bright, our hearts can bloom with love. So, let's be gentle and sweet, filling our day with loving actions. Remember, when we love like Jesus, we make the world a happier place!

Reflection:

What is something kind you can do today to show love, just like Jesus? Maybe you can share a toy or give a friend a hug. How will that make you feel?

Today's Prayer:

Dear Jesus, thank you for teaching us to love each other like you love us. Help me to share hugs and smiles, spreading happiness and kindness all around!

13
JANUARY

God's Promises are True
God keeps His promises because He loves us!
(Psalm 145:13)

Lucia and Mia love to play! Sometimes, Lucia feels scared of big shadows. Mom says, "God is with you, so don't be afraid!" Lucia steps into the sunshine with Mia. Like Lucia, we can trust God to keep us safe. When you feel scared, remember—God is always with you, giving courage and comfort!

Reflection:

Can you show me what you do to feel brave when you're scared, knowing that God always keeps His promises and stays with you?

Today's Prayer:

Dear God, thank you for always keeping your promises and staying with me when I feel scared. Please help me remember your love and feel brave, knowing you are always by my side.

14 JANUARY

Forgiveness: Saying Sorry and Making Things Right

Be kind and tender-hearted, forgiving one another, just as God forgave you. (Ephesians 4:32)

Once, there was a little girl named Lily who played with her friend Emma. One day, Lily accidentally knocked over Emma's favorite toy, and it broke. Lily felt sad and knew she needed to say "sorry." So, she went to Emma, gave her a big hug, and said sorry. Emma smiled and said, "It's okay, let's play together!" They both felt happy again!

Reflection:

What do you think it feels like when you say you're sorry? Can you think of a time when you made a friend feel better by saying sorry?

Today's Prayer:

Dear God, thank you for helping us say sorry when we hurt others. Please help us always to love each other and make things right again. Amen.

---

15 JANUARY

Faith Over Fear

God is with me, so I don't need to be scared!
(Isaiah 41:10)

A little squirrel saw big, wiggly shadows and felt afraid. But she remembered, "God is with me!" Taking a deep breath, she flicked her tail and scampered ahead. The shadows were just branches! She laughed, feeling brave. When you're scared, remember—God is always with you!

Reflection:

When you feel a little scared like the squirrel in the cozy forest, what makes you feel brave and safe? Can you think of something special about God that helps you feel warm and happy inside?

Today's Prayer:

Dear God, thank you for staying with me when I feel scared. Please help me remember you are always near and help me feel brave inside.

16 JANUARY

Being Honest and Truthful
Always tell the truth, little one!
(Ephesians 4:25)

A small bluebird loved to chirp and play in the trees. One day, a cardinal shared his juicy berries. The bluebird wanted to feel special, so he said he had some too—even though he didn't! The cardinal looked surprised. Then the bluebird remembered, "Always tell the truth!" He chirped, "I don't have any berries." The cardinal smiled, and they shared happily. Telling the truth brings joy and keeps friendships bright!

Reflection:

Can you show me how you tell the truth, even when it's hard, just like the little bluebird did with his friend?

Today's Prayer:

Dear God, thank you for helping me tell the truth, even when it's hard. Please help me be honest and keep my friendships happy and bright.

---

17 JANUARY

Jesus' Miracles and Power
Jesus can do amazing things!
(John 14:12)

Jesus walked on water, healed the sick, and even turned water into yummy juice! He is powerful and full of love. One day, He said, "You can do amazing things too!" Just like a superhero! When you feel scared or need help, remember—Jesus is with you, ready to do something amazing. Trust Him, little one, and let His love shine in your heart!

Reflection:

What is something special you can do today to help someone feel happy, just like how Jesus helps us?

Today's Prayer:

Dear Jesus, thank you for loving me and doing amazing things. Please help me trust you and share your love with others every day.

18
JANUARY

God's Plan for You
God loves you and has a special plan for you!
(Jeremiah 29:11)

A little deer loved running through the meadow. One day, she tripped and knocked over a basket of berries. She felt embarrassed but took a deep breath and said, "I spilled them." Her friends smiled and helped her clean up. The deer felt warm inside, knowing honesty is part of God's special plan. Remember, little one, God loves you and has a wonderful plan just for you!

Reflection:

What makes you feel warm and happy inside, just like the little deer when she was honest with her friends?

Today's Prayer:

Dear God, thank you for loving me like a warm hug and for having a special plan just for me. Help me to be brave and honest, knowing you are always there, just like the little deer with her friends.

19
JANUARY

Being a Light in the World
You are a light that shines bright!
(Matthew 5:14)

Faye loved to shine bright, just like a twinkling star! One day, she shared her toy with a friend and smiled. "You are a light that shines bright!" her friend said. Faye felt warm inside, knowing kindness makes the world sparkle. When you share love and joy, you shine too! Keep shining, little one!

Reflection:

Can you show me how you shine bright by sharing or being kind to someone, just like Faye did?

Today's Prayer:

Dear God, thank you for helping me shine bright with kindness and love. Please help me share and be a light to everyone around me.

20 JANUARY

Heaven is a Wonderful Place

Heaven is a happy home with God, where we are loved! (John 14:2)

God made a beautiful home in heaven, full of joy and love! Just like flowers bloom and stars shine, you are special to Him. Heaven is a happy place where His love never ends. When you laugh, play, or feel shy, remember—God's love is always with you. One day, His wonderful home will be ready for you, shining with joy!

Reflection:

Can you show me how you feel when you think about God's happy home in heaven, where you are always loved?

Today's Prayer:

Dear God, thank You for making a beautiful home in Heaven where Your love shines bright. Help me to always feel Your joy in my heart, knowing that I am special to You.

---

21 JANUARY

Respecting and Loving Others

Love each other, just like I love you! (John 15:12)

Jesus was kind and full of love. He healed the sick and made people happy with His miracles. But most of all, He taught us to love one another! He showed kindness to everyone, big or small. When you share, help, or give a hug, you are sharing His love too. Remember, little one, loving others makes the world brighter—just like Jesus taught us!

Reflection:

Think about a time when you shared your toys or gave someone a hug. How did that make you feel? Can you think of someone you can show love to today, just like Jesus did?

Today's Prayer:

Dear Jesus, thank you for loving me and showing me how to be kind. Please help me share your love with others by being gentle and caring every day.

22 JANUARY

God Created Everything
God made the sky, the trees, and you too!
(Genesis 1:31)

Once upon a time, in a world of wonder, God painted the sky blue and filled it with fluffy clouds. He made tall trees to play under and flowers that dance in the breeze. And He made you, too! You are a special part of God's creation, just like the stars and butterflies. Whenever you see a beautiful flower or hear a bird sing, remember: God made everything and loves you very much!

Reflection:

Can you point to something beautiful around you, like a flower or a tree, and say, "Thank you, God, for making this and for making me!"?

Today's Prayer:

Dear God, thank you for making the sky, the trees, and me. Please help me remember how much you love everything you made.

---

23 JANUARY

Being a Good Friend
Be kind to others.
(Ephesians 4:32)

Keila loved to play! One day, she saw a girl sitting alone and remembered Jesus wants us to be kind. She sat beside her, shared a toy, and asked, "Want to play?" The girl smiled, and soon they were giggling together.

Kindness grows friendships! Being a good friend fills our hearts with joy and spreads God's love!

Reflection:

Can you show me how you can be a good friend by sharing or inviting someone to play with you, just like Keila did?

Today's Prayer:

Dear God, thank you for my friends and for teaching me to be kind. Please help me share and invite others to play, so I can be a good friend too.

24
JANUARY

God's Strength in Difficult Times
God is our helper when we are scared.
(Psalm 46:1)

Victoria loved playing under the trees, but one day, a storm came. Thunder rumbled, and she felt scared. Then she remembered—God made trees strong, and He made her strong too! She whispered a prayer and felt peace.

When the storm passed, she smiled, knowing God is always with her. Whenever you're afraid, remember—God keeps you safe!

Reflection:

Can you show me what helps you feel safe and strong when you're scared, just like Victoria remembered God is always with her?

Today's Prayer:

Dear God, thank you for making me strong and helping me when I feel scared. Please stay with me and help me feel safe and brave every day.

25
JANUARY

Speaking with Kind Words
Kind words are like sunshine!
(Proverbs 16:24)

Hazel and Rose loved playing together! One day, Hazel saw Rose looking sad. Instead of playing alone, she sat beside her and said, "I'm here for you." Rose smiled. Hazel shared her teddy bear and said, "You are my special friend!" Rose's frown turned into giggles, and soon they were laughing and hugging. Kind words make hearts happy, just like sunshine. Let's use kind words to spread love and joy!

Reflection:

Can you show me how you use kind words to make someone smile, just like Hazel did for Rose?

Today's Prayer:

Dear God, thank you for teaching me to use kind words. Please help me make others happy and share your love with my words every day.

26
JANUARY

Jesus Teaches Us to Serve
Jesus loves when we help each other!
(Mark 10:45)

A little Kitten loved playing in the sunshine. One day, she saw her friend struggling to carry a heavy basket. Instead of running off to play, she stopped to help. Together, they carried the basket, and her friend smiled. The Kitten felt happy inside, Knowing she had shared love through Kindness. Jesus teaches us to help others with a joyful heart, making the world a brighter place!

Reflection:

What do you think it feels like when you help a friend, just like the little Kitten helped her friend with the heavy basket?

Today's Prayer:

Dear Jesus, thank you for teaching us to help our friends like the little Kitten who shared love and Kindness. Please fill our hearts with joy as we serve others and make the world a happier place.

27
JANUARY

Helping the Poor and Those in Need
Helping others makes God happy!
(Acts 20:35)

In a colorful garden, a sweet flower named Daisy loved to help others. She provided shade to tired ants and shared her petals with a hungry bee. Each time she helped, her heart felt warm and bright. Just like sunshine brings joy, helping others fills hearts with love. When we share and care for those in need, we make the world a happier place. Kindness makes God smile!

Reflection:

Can you show me how you help someone or share with a friend, just like Daisy helped the ants and the bee?

 ### Today's Prayer:

Dear God, thank you for giving me ways to help and share with others. Please help me be Kind and make you smile by caring for those who need it.

28
JANUARY

Being Thankful Every Day
Give thanks to God for all the good things!
(Psalm 136:1)

Jesus saw His friends feeling hungry, so He shared His loaves and fish, filling their hearts with joy. Just like Jesus, we can be thankful for what we have and share with others! A smile, a hug, or a kind word shows gratitude for God's blessings. When we say "thank you" and appreciate the good things around us, our hearts shine with joy. Remember, little one, a thankful heart makes every day brighter!

Reflection:

What is something nice you can share with a friend today that makes you feel happy and thankful?

Today's Prayer:

Dear God, thank you for all the good things you give me. Please help me share and say "thank you" with a happy heart every day.

29
JANUARY

God is Always With You
Where can I go from Your Spirit? Where can I flee from Your presence? (Psalm 139:7)

Once upon a time, there was a little girl named Diana who loved to explore. One day, as she peeked behind colorful flowers, she felt a warm hug. It was God, saying, "I'm with you wherever you go!" Diana giggled, knowing she wasn't alone. As she danced with butterflies and climbed tall trees, she remembered that God was always by her side, like a special friend. So, little one, wherever you play, God is always with you!

Reflection:

Can you show me how you feel happy and safe knowing God is with you wherever you go, just like Diana did when she played and explored?

Today's Prayer:

Dear God, thank you for being with me wherever I go. Please help me feel happy and safe, knowing you are always by my side.

30
JANUARY

Learning to Be Patient

Wait for the Lord; be strong and take heart and wait for the Lord. (Psalm 27:14)

Denise woke up smiling. One morning, she saw flower buds and wanted them to bloom immediately. She remembered flowers need time to grow, so she waited patiently. Soon, they bloomed beautifully. Denise learned that good things happen when we wait. Patience brings wonderful surprises, just like flowers blooming in time!

Reflection:

Can you show me how you wait patiently for something special, just like Denise waited for the flowers to bloom?

Today's Prayer:

Dear God, thank you for teaching me to wait patiently. Please help me remember that good things come when I wait and trust you.

31
JANUARY

Courage and Standing Up for What's Right

Be strong and brave; God is with you!

(Joshua 1:9)

Olivia loved to play, but one day, she saw a friend treated unkindly. Nervous, she wondered if she should speak up. Then she remembered, "God helps me be brave!" Taking a deep breath, she said, "Let's be kind." Her words made a difference! Olivia felt strong, knowing trusting God gives us courage to do what's right!

Reflection:

Can you show me how you can be brave and use kind words to help someone, just like Olivia did?

Today's Prayer:

Dear God, thank you for helping me be brave and do what's right. Please help me use kind words and stand up for others, knowing you are always with me.

February

1
FEBRUARY

The Power of Worship and Praise
God loves to hear our happy songs!
(Psalm 100:1)

Celine loved singing in her garden. Her songs made the flowers sway and birds chirp along. She twirled in the sunlight, full of joy!

One day, she learned—God loves hearing her songs! So, every time she sang, she shared her heart with Him. Her music filled the air with love, reminding her that worship is a beautiful gift to God!

Reflection:

When you sing your happy songs in the garden, how do you think the flowers and birds feel? What is your favorite song to sing for God?

———————— ⸙ ————————

Today's Prayer:

Dear God, thank you for loving my happy songs. Please help me sing to you with a joyful heart every day.

2
FEBRUARY

God's Rules Keep Us Safe
God's rules help us do what's right and keep us safe. (Psalm 119:105)

Tina the turtle loved to explore! One day, she followed a shiny butterfly too far. "Tina, stay close!" called Mommy Turtle. She stopped and returned, realizing Mommy's rules kept her safe. God's rules do the same! They guide and protect us. Like Tina, we can trust that following God's ways keeps us safe and happy!

Reflection:

What do you think happens when we listen to Mommy Turtle's rules, just like Tina did? How do those rules help us stay safe while we explore?

———————— ⸙ ————————

Today's Prayer:

Dear God, thank you for giving us rules to help keep us safe and happy. Please help me listen and follow your ways every day.

3 FEBRUARY

Loving Others from a Full Heart

Love everyone with a big heart!
(1 John 4:7)

Aria loved playing in the colorful garden, hopping around with joy. She shared her favorite berries with friends and gave the sweetest hugs. A wise turtle told her, "Loving others comes from a big heart!" So, Aria filled her heart with kindness and smiled at everyone. When you love like Aria, your heart shines bright, and happiness spreads everywhere!

Reflection:

Can you think of a time when you shared something or gave a hug to a friend? How did it make you feel inside your big heart?

❧

Today's Prayer:

Dear God, thank you for filling my heart with love. Please help me share kindness and hugs with everyone, so my heart can shine bright for you.

---

4 FEBRUARY

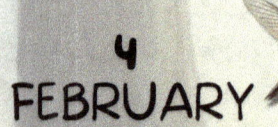

Waiting Well with God

God is with you while you wait, and He loves you so much! (Psalm 27:14)

Nora, a little hummingbird, wanted to fly high in the sky. But first, she had to wait for her wings to grow strong. She felt a bit sad, but she remembered God was with her. "I love you, Nora," whispered God. So, she chirped and danced while she waited. When her wings were ready, she soared above the trees! Waiting is joyful when we trust God's love!

Reflection:

Can you show me how you wait with a happy heart, just like Nora did while her wings grew strong?

❧

Today's Prayer:

Dear God, thank you for being with me while I wait. Please help me have a happy heart and trust your love every day.

5
FEBRUARY

Letting Go of Control
God cares for you, so let go and be happy!
(1 Peter 5:7)

Layla, a little hedgehog, loved to hold her toys tightly, afraid to share. One day, her friend the wise old owl said, "Layla, when you let go of your toys, more fun comes! God cares for you, so let go and be happy." Layla took a deep breath and shared. Joy filled the air as all her friends played together. Like Layla, you can let go and trust God to fill your heart with happiness!

Reflection:
Can you show me how you let go and share your toys, just like Layla did, and see how much fun you can have with your friends?

Today's Prayer:
Dear God, thank you for caring for me and filling my heart with happiness. Please help me let go and share with my friends, trusting you to bring us joy.

6
FEBRUARY

God's Mercy Is New Each Morning
Every morning, God gives us new love!
(Lamentations 3:22-23)

Abby woke up and stretched her arms wide. She saw the sunshine peeking through her window and felt happy inside. Every day, God gives Abby a fresh start, just like a brand-new day! Even if Abby made a mistake yesterday, God's love is still there, warm and gentle. Abby can smile and know that God's mercy is always new. She can try again, laugh, and feel God's love in her heart every single day.

Reflection:
Can you show me your biggest smile and tell me how you feel when you remember that God gives you new love every day?

Today's Prayer:
Dear God, thank you for giving me new love every day. Please help me remember your love is always with me, no matter what.

7
FEBRUARY

God is a Safe Place When We're Afraid
When I am afraid, God is with me.
(Psalm 56:3)

A little ladybug named Ruby hid under a leaf as the wind whistled through the backyard garden. She felt so small and afraid. "God, are you here?" she whispered. Just then, a raindrop sparkled in the sunlight, and Ruby felt warm inside. She knew God was watching over her. Taking a deep breath, she crawled out, feeling safe. When you're scared, remember—God is always with you!

Reflection:
Can you show me how you feel safe and brave when you remember that God is with you, just like Ruby the ladybug did?

— ❧ —

Today's Prayer:
Dear God, thank you for being with me when I feel scared. Please help me feel safe and brave, knowing you are always by my side.

•

8
FEBRUARY

The Parable of the Lost Sheep: Jesus Cares for You
God loves you like a shepherd loves his sheep.
(John 10:14)

Mia, a little lamb, loved to skip through the garden. One day, she wandered too far and felt lost. "Shepherd, where are you?" she cried. Then, she heard his gentle voice. He scooped her up and whispered, "I'll always find you." Mia snuggled close, feeling safe and loved. Sweet girl, just like the shepherd loves Mia, Jesus always cares for you!

Reflection:
Can you show me how you feel safe and loved when someone takes care of you, just like Mia felt with her shepherd?

— ❧ —

Today's Prayer:

Dear Jesus, thank you for always caring for me and keeping me safe. Please help me remember that you love me just like a shepherd loves his little sheep.

9 FEBRUARY

The Parable of the Good Samaritan: Helping Others
Let's be nice and help others, just like the Good Samaritan did! (Luke 10:25-37)

Annie saw a girl fall while playing in the garden. She ran over and said, "I will help!" She gave her a hug, wiped her tears, and held her hand. Soon, the girl smiled again! Just like the Good Samaritan, Annie showed kindness. When we help, share, or give a hug, we show love too! Sweet girl, kindness makes our hearts happy. Let's be like Annie and help others!

Reflection:

When you see a friend who feels sad or hurt, how do you like to help them feel better, just like Annie did? Can you think of a time when you helped someone? What did you do?

Today's Prayer:

Dear God, thank you for helping us be kind like the Good Samaritan. Please help us share love and hugs, just like Annie did, so everyone can smile again.

---

10 FEBRUARY

Your Life Still Has Purpose
You are special and loved by God!
(Psalm 139:14)

Llyana loved to twirl in her favorite dress and sing her happy song. Sometimes, she wondered if she was important. But God made Llyana special, with a big heart and a bright smile! Even when she feels small, God has a special plan just for her. Llyana's hugs, giggles, and kindness make the world better. God smiles when He sees Llyana being herself, because she is wonderfully made and loved every single day.

Reflection:

Can you show me your happy dance or big smile, knowing that God made you special and loves you every day?

Today's Prayer:

Dear God, thank you for making me special and loving me every day. Please help me remember that I am important to you and can share your love with others.

11 FEBRUARY

God's Creation: Taking Care of the Earth
God made the world, and we can love it
and take care of it! (Genesis 1:31)

Maddie ran outside, twirling in the sunshine. "Look at the trees and flowers!" she cheered. God made the world so beautiful!

She picked up a piece of paper, saying, "Now the earth is happy!" When we care for God's world—watering flowers, loving animals, and keeping it clean—we show our love for Him. Let's care for His creation together!

Reflection:

Can you show me how you help take care of God's world, like picking up trash or watering flowers, just like Maddie did?

Today's Prayer:

Dear God, thank you for making our beautiful world. Please help me take care of your creation by loving the earth and keeping it clean.

---

12 FEBRUARY

Jesus Calms the Storm: Trusting Him in Hard Times
Jesus helps us feel safe, even when
things are scary. (Mark 4:39)

Millie watched dark clouds roll in. BOOM! Thunder made her jump. "Mommy, I'm scared!" she said. Mommy held her close. "Let's talk to Jesus," she whispered. Millie closed her eyes. "Jesus, I'm trusting You." The rain slowed, and she felt safe. Just like Jesus calmed the storm, He helps us feel brave and brings us peace!

Reflection:

Can you show me how you feel safe and calm when you talk to Jesus, just like Millie did during the storm?

Today's Prayer:

Dear Jesus, thank you for helping me feel safe when I am scared. Please stay close to me and bring me peace, just like you did for Millie.

13
FEBRUARY

The Fruits of the Spirit
Love, joy, and peace are from God, and they make us happy! (Galatians 5:22)

Once upon a time, in a sunny garden, there lived three special friends: Love, Joy, and Peace. Love gave the best hugs that made everyone feel warm inside. Joy danced around with laughter, making flowers bloom brightly. Peace quietly wrapped everyone in a cozy blanket, calming their hearts. When we share Love, Joy, and Peace, we feel happy, just like in God's garden! So, let's play, hug, and smile together, spreading these sweet fruits all day long!

Reflection:

Can you show me how you share love, joy, or peace with others, like giving a hug, dancing, or helping someone feel calm?

Today's Prayer:

Dear God, thank you for giving me love, joy, and peace. Please help me share these sweet gifts with everyone around me every day.

14
FEBRUARY

God's Love That Never Fails
God loves you always, and His love never ends! (Psalm 136:1)

Sophie twirled in her pink dress, holding a heart-shaped card. "This is for you, Mommy!" she said, smiling. Mommy hugged her. "Thank you, sweetheart! God's love is the biggest of all." Sophie ran to the garden, telling the flowers and her teddy, "God loves you!" She knew God's love was always with her, forever and ever!

Reflection:

Can you show me how you share God's love with someone, like giving a hug or saying "I love you," just like Sophie did?

Today's Prayer:

Dear God, thank you for loving me forever. Please help me share your love with others every day.

15 FEBRUARY

God Hears Your Prayers
God listens when you talk to Him!
(1 John 5:14)

Hannah loved talking to God. She whispered her dreams and told Him about her day. One morning, she asked, "God, will You help my flower grow?" She watered it and waited. Soon, a tiny bud appeared! Hannah clapped, knowing God heard her. Just like Hannah, you can talk to God anytime—He listens, He cares, and He loves you so much!

Reflection:

What is something special you would like to tell God today, just like Hannah did? Can you show me how you talk to God and know He is listening to you?

Today's Prayer:

Dear God, thank you for always listening when I talk to you. Please help me remember that you care about everything I say and love me very much.

---

16 FEBRUARY

Being Joyful in All Situations
Be happy and smile every day!
(Psalm 118:24)

Joy loved to dance, sing, and play every day! One sunny day, she tripped and fell. But instead of being sad, she giggled and laughed. "I can be happy even when I fall!" she thought. Just like Joy, we can choose to smile, even when things aren't perfect. Remember, every day is a gift from God! Let's spread our smiles everywhere we go!

Reflection:

Can you show me your happiest smile or a silly dance, even when something doesn't go just right, just like Joy did?

Today's Prayer:

Dear God, thank you for giving me happy days and helping me smile, even when things are hard. Please help me share my joy with others every day.

17
FEBRUARY

Giving Cheerfully
God loves a happy giver!
(2 Corinthians 9:7)

A little girl named Jasmine loved to share her toys with her friends. When she gave them away, she would giggle with joy! One day, she remembered, "God loves a happy giver!" So, Jasmine smiled and shared even more. Her friends were so happy, and Jasmine's heart felt warm and bright. Sharing makes us smile, just like Jasmine, because giving cheerfully brings love to everyone!

Reflection:

Can you show me how you share something with a big smile, just like Jasmine did when she gave her toys to her friends?

Today's Prayer:

Dear God, thank you for giving me good things to share. Please help me give to others with a happy heart and a big smile.

18
FEBRUARY

God's Love Never Ends
God loves us forever and ever!
(Psalm 136:1)

Nina loved to play and laugh, always knowing that God was with her. One day, she picked a daisy and whispered, "God loves me forever and ever!" Just like the bright sun and the cozy hugs from her family, God's love is always there. No matter where she goes, God's love never ends!

Reflection:

Can you show me how you feel when you remember that God loves you forever, just like Nina did with her daisy?

Today's Prayer:

Dear God, thank you for loving me forever and ever. Please help me remember your love is always with me, no matter where I go.

19 FEBRUARY

God is Our Protector
God is like a big hug, keeping us safe.
(Psalm 46:1)

Kesha loved to explore, and one day, she saw a big bear! But instead of being scared, she remembered that God is like a big hug, keeping her safe. She smiled and said, "God, thank you for hugging me!" Just like a cozy blanket, God wraps us in love and keeps us safe, always nearby.

Reflection:

When you think about how God keeps you safe like a big hug, what makes you feel cozy and loved, just like Kesha felt when she saw the big bear?

Today's Prayer:

Dear God, thank you for wrapping me in your love and keeping me safe. Please help me remember you are always with me, like a big, warm hug.

---

20 FEBRUARY

Spreading God's Love
Love each other like God loves you!
(1 John 4:7)

Vanessa, a little butterfly, loved to share her beautiful colors with everyone. She fluttered around, giving warm hugs to the flowers, making them bloom brighter. One day, she heard a gentle whisper: "Love each other like God loves you!" Vanessa sprinkled her love everywhere, making the world a happier place!

Reflection:

Can you think of a time when you shared your smiles or hugs with someone? How did it make them feel, just like Vanessa the butterfly sharing her love?

Today's Prayer:

Dear God, thank you for showing me how to share your love with others. Please help me spread kindness and make the world a happier place every day.

21 FEBRUARY

Telling Others About Jesus
Go tell your friends about Jesus' love!
(Mark 16:15)

Agnes smiled big, knowing Jesus' love. One sunny day, she told her friends, "Did you know Jesus loves you?" They giggled and listened. Sharing Jesus' love is like giving hugs! Like Agnes, we can spread joy and tell everyone about Jesus' love today, tomorrow, and always!

Reflection:

If you were giving hugs to everyone you love, how would you tell them that Jesus loves them too?

Today's Prayer:

Dear Jesus, thank you for your love that makes us smile and feel happy. Help us to share your love with our friends, just like Agnes did, so they can feel your joy too!

---

22 FEBRUARY

Jesus' Love for Children
Jesus loves the little children!
(Mark 10:14)

Jesus saw children playing and said, "Come to me! I love you!" His love is like a warm hug, wrapping around us all.
Imagine Jesus holding your hand, skipping through a sunny garden, saying, "You are so special!" Remember, Jesus loves you more than anything! You are His little star, shining bright just as you are!

Reflection:

Can you pretend you are holding Jesus' hand and skipping through a sunny garden? What do you feel in your heart when you think about how much He loves you?

Today's Prayer:

Dear Jesus, thank you for loving me so much and for always being my friend. Help me feel your warm hugs and know that I am your special little star!

23 FEBRUARY

Following Jesus Every Day
Jesus loves you and will always be with you! (Matthew 28:20)

Molly loved to play in the sunshine, pick flowers, and dance with butterflies. Every day, she remembered that Jesus loves her and is always with her. When she giggled, Jesus giggled with her. When she felt shy, He gave her a warm hug. Just like Molly, you can hold Jesus in your heart. So, let's skip joyfully, knowing Jesus loves us and is with us all day long!

Reflection:

Can you show me how you feel happy knowing Jesus is with you all day, just like Molly felt when she played and danced?

Today's Prayer:

Dear Jesus, thank you for being with me every day and loving me so much. Please help me remember you are always close, no matter where I go.

---

24 FEBRUARY

Loving Your Siblings
Love one another just like I love you! (John 15:12)

Ava and her baby brother Sam loved to play together. One sunny day, Ava shared her favorite toy with Sam. "I love you like Jesus loves us!" she said with a smile. Sam giggled, happy to play. When they hugged each other, their hearts felt warm and snuggly. Love makes us happy! Let's share love every day!

Reflection:

Can you think of a time when you shared a toy with your siblings and it made you all smile? How did sharing make your hearts feel?

Today's Prayer:

Dear Jesus, thank you for teaching me to love my family. Please help me share and be kind to my brother or sister, just like you love us.

25
FEBRUARY

God Gives Us Wisdom

God gives us wise and happy hearts!
(Proverbs 2:6)

Camila loved exploring her sunny garden, playing with butterflies and flowers. One day, she asked a friendly owl, "How can I always make good choices?" The wise owl smiled and said, "God helps us with His love and wisdom!" Camila beamed, knowing that with Jesus by her side, she could always choose the right path.

Reflection:

Can you show me how you make a good choice, like sharing or being kind, knowing that God helps you be wise just like Camila?

Today's Prayer:

Dear God, thank you for helping me make good choices every day. Please fill my heart with your wisdom and love so I can do what is right.

26
FEBRUARY

God Created Families

God made families to love each other!
(Genesis 1:27)

God made something very special—families! Sandra's family loved each other so much. They played games, laughed together, and gave warm hugs. Every time they helped and smiled, they were showing God's love. Sandra knew that Jesus was always with her and her family, keeping them close and full of joy!

Reflection:

Can you think of a favorite time when you played or hugged with your family? How did that make you feel like God was with you?

Today's Prayer:

Dear God, thank You for our special family who loves each other so much. Help us to play, laugh, and hug, sharing Your love every day!

27 FEBRUARY

Showing Compassion Like Jesus

Be kind and love everyone, just like Jesus!
(Ephesians 4:32)

Liz saw her friend Tamara with a scraped knee and feeling sad. Remembering how Jesus was kind, Liz smiled and said, "It's okay to feel sad."
She gently helped Tamara, kissed her knee, and gave her teddy bear. "Jesus loves us and helps us when we're sad," Liz said. Like Jesus, Liz showed love and kindness, making both hearts happy!

Reflection:

When you see a friend feeling sad, what nice thing can you do to help them feel better, just like Liz helped Tamara?

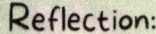

Today's Prayer:

Dear Jesus, thank you for showing me how to be kind and loving. Please help me care for my friends and make them feel better when they are sad.

---

28 FEBRUARY

Using Our Gifts to Honor God

Use your hands to help and be a friend!
(1 Peter 4:10)

Jill loves to color with her crayons and build tall towers with her blocks. God gives Jill special hands to do wonderful things! When Jill shares her toys or helps a friend, she uses her gifts to make God smile. Even little hands do big things when they are kind and helpful. Every day, Jill uses her hands to show love, help others, and be a good friend, just like God wants!

Reflection:

Can you show me how you use your hands to help someone or share, just like Jill does with her toys and blocks?

Today's Prayer:

Dear God, thank you for giving me special hands to help and share. Please help me use my hands to show love and make you smile every day.

March

1
MARCH

God's Love for You
God loves you so much!
(1 John 4:9)

Lily loves to play outside, hugging her teddy bear and feeling God's love. As she runs around, she notices the flowers blooming and butterflies dancing, and she remembers that all of nature is loved by God. It fills her heart with happiness to see how beautiful His world is.

Are you wearing a happy smile today? You are special and deeply loved by God! Whether you're feeling joyful or a little sad, always remember that God loves you more than anything! You are His shining star, and He wants you to be happy every day.

Reflection:

Can you show me your happy smile and tell me what makes you feel loved by God, just like Lily does when she plays outside?

Today's Prayer:

Dear God, thank you for loving me so much and making me your shining star. Please help me feel your love every day and share my happy smile with others.

2 MARCH

Honoring God with Our Actions

Do what makes God happy!
(Psalm 100:2)

In a red barn, Penelope the lamb loved to play. One sunny day, a wise horse said, "Do what makes God happy!" Penelope shared her hay, helped a chick, and nuzzled a sleepy cow. Each act of kindness filled her heart with joy. Like Penelope, you can honor God by being kind and making the world a happier place!

Reflection:

How do you feel when you do something kind for a friend, just like Penelope shared her hay and helped others?

Today's Prayer:

Dear God, thank you for sunny days and the joy of being kind like Penelope the lamb. Help me to share and care, so my actions can make you happy.

---

3 MARCH

Becoming a Vessel of Grace

God loves you very much, and you can share His love with others! (1 John 4:19)

In a bright and colorful garden, there lived a gentle little fawn named Willow. Every day, she pranced through the meadows, sharing joy with her sweet smile. One sunny morning, she found a tired ladybug and helped her find a cozy leaf to rest on. Just like Willow, you can share God's love, too! Your hugs are like sunshine, making everyone feel happy. Remember, your love is a special gift you can share with all your friends!

Reflection:

When you see a friend feeling sad or tired, what kind of sunshine can you share with them, just like Willow does in the garden?

Today's Prayer:

Dear God, thank you for letting me share your love with others. Please help me be like Willow and bring sunshine and kindness to my friends every day.

4
MARCH

Learning to Depend on Him
God loves you and helps you every day!
(Psalm 46:1)

Elena the little monkey wanted to climb the tallest tree but felt a bit scared. She heard a soft voice in her heart, "I love you!" It was God, reminding her He was always with her. With each little leap, Elena grew braver. Soon, she climbed all the way to the top, feeling loved and strong. Just like Elena, you can always count on God to help you grow and feel safe!

Reflection:

Can you think of a time when you felt a little scared, just like Elena the monkey? What do you like to do when you remember that God is with you and loves you?

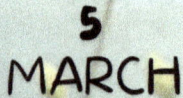

Today's Prayer:

Dear God, thank you for loving me and helping me be brave. Please stay with me and help me grow strong every day.

5
MARCH

God's Timing Is Perfect
God knows when the right time is for everything! (Ecclesiastes 3:1)

In a sunny garden, a little flower dreamed of dancing with the breeze. "Oh, how I wish to sway!" she sighed. The wise gardener said, "Dear flower, wait. God knows the perfect time for you to bloom!" The flower giggled, trusting his words. She waited patiently, knowing she'd dance beautifully in time. We can trust God has a lovely plan for us!

Reflection:

If you were a little flower in the garden, what would you do while you wait to dance with the breeze? Would you sing, play, or watch the clouds?

Today's Prayer:

Dear God, thank you for knowing the perfect time for everything in my life. Please help me wait patiently and trust your plan while I grow.

6
MARCH

You Are Not Alone

God is always with you, so you are never alone!
(Isaiah 41:10)

Leah the little Koala wanted to climb high like the others, but she felt small and unsure. As she hugged the tree, she heard a gentle whisper, "I am with you!" It was God, reminding her she was never alone. With each little step, Leah felt braver. Soon, she reached the top, feeling safe and loved. Just like Leah, remember—God is always with you!

Reflection:

Can you show me how you feel brave and safe knowing God is with you, just like Leah did when she climbed the tree?

Today's Prayer:

Dear God, thank you for being with me so I am never alone. Please help me feel brave and safe every day, knowing you are always by my side.

7
MARCH

Abiding in the Vine

God loves you, and when you stay close to Him, you grow big and strong like a pretty flower! (John 15:5)

A little chipmunk named Sadie loved to scamper up her favorite tree. The strong branches kept her safe and held her tight. "I love my tree!" Sadie chirped happily. Just like Sadie stays close to her tree, we stay close to God. He helps us grow strong and joyful! Remember, sweet one, God loves you and holds you close every day!

Reflection:

Can you think of something that makes you feel safe and happy, just like Sadie loves her tree?

Today's Prayer:

Dear God, thank you for holding me close and helping me grow strong. Please help me stay near you and feel your love every day.

8 MARCH

Trusting Through Transitions

God is with you wherever you go!
(Psalm 139:10)

In a bright garden, a little bee felt nervous—it was her first time flying far from the hive! A wise owl gently said, "Don't be afraid! God is always with you." Taking a deep breath, she flapped her tiny wings and soared into the sky. She smiled, knowing she was never alone. Like the little bee, you can trust God in every new adventure!

Reflection:

Can you think of a time when you were trying something new, like the little bee? What helped you feel brave and happy to try it?

Today's Prayer:

Dear God, thank you for being with me in all my adventures, just like you are with the little bee. Help me to trust and be brave, knowing you are always by my side, no matter where I go.

---

9 MARCH

Choosing Peace in Uncertainty

God gives us peace in our hearts, even when things are unsure. (Philippians 4:7)

A little dragonfly felt a flutter in her wings, unsure of where to fly next. She remembered that God gives peace, even when things feel uncertain. Taking a deep breath, she gently fluttered her wings and found a peaceful spot to rest. Choosing peace helped her feel safe, knowing God was with her always.

Reflection:

What is your favorite way to take a deep breath and find a peaceful spot, just like the little dragonfly?

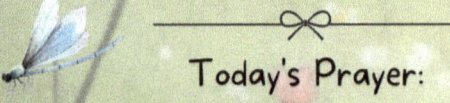

Today's Prayer:

Dear God, thank you for your peace in our hearts, just like the dragonfly who flutters gently. Help us to find a safe place and trust you, even when we're unsure.

10
MARCH

Holding On to God's Promises
God's promises are like a warm hug for us!
(Isaiah 41:10)

Natalie loved hugs, especially from her mommy. One day, while playing outside, she felt a gentle breeze and heard a soft whisper: "God's promises are like a warm hug for you!" She smiled, thinking of all the times God promised to be with her. Each promise felt cozy, like a big bear hug. Whenever she felt scared, she squeezed her heart and held on to those warm promises.

Reflection:

Can you think of a time when you felt a warm hug from mommy? How does that hug make you feel, just like God's promises?

Today's Prayer:

Dear God, thank you for your promises that make me feel safe and loved. Please help me remember your hugs and hold your promises close to my heart every day.

11
MARCH

Letting God Define Your Worth
You are precious and loved just as you are!
(Isaiah 43:4)

A little moth hid in the shadows, watching the bright butterflies dance in the sun. "I'm not as pretty as they are," she sighed. Then, a gentle voice whispered, "You are precious and loved just as you are!" Warmth filled her heart. She fluttered her wings with joy, knowing God made her just right. Sweet friend, you are special too—God loves you every day!

Reflection:

What's something special about you that makes you happy, just like the little moth learned she is special to God?

Today's Prayer:

Dear God, thank you for making me special and loving me just as I am. Please help me remember that I am precious to you every day.

12 MARCH

Encouragement for the Weary Soul
Jesus loves you and makes you strong!
(Isaiah 40:29)

A little beetle peeked from under a leaf, her shiny wings feeling heavy. "I'm too small to keep going," she sighed. Then, a gentle breeze whispered, "Jesus loves you and makes you strong!" She took a deep breath, stretched her wings, and felt new strength inside. With a happy flutter, she scurried ahead. Sweet friend, you are loved and strong too!

Reflection:
When you feel tired like the little beetle, what is something you can say to yourself to remember that you are loved and strong?

Today's Prayer:
Dear Jesus, thank you for loving me and giving me strength when I feel tired. Help me remember your love makes me brave and helps me keep going, even when things feel hard.

---

13 MARCH

When You Feel Spiritually Stuck
God is always with you, helping you to grow like a little flower! (Matthew 28:20)

A little sunflower stretched toward the sky. "I want to grow, but I feel stuck," she sighed. Then, a gentle whisper surrounded her, "I am with you!" It was God! With each sunbeam and raindrop, she felt stronger. Just like the sunflower, when you feel stuck, remember God is helping you grow. Close your eyes and know His love is always shining on you!

Reflection:
Can you show me how you reach up high like a sunflower, knowing God is helping you grow, even when things feel a little hard?

Today's Prayer:
Dear God, thank you for staying with me and helping me grow, even when I feel stuck. Please shine your love on me and help me reach for you, just like a sunflower reaching for the sun.

14 MARCH

Faith That Moves Mountains

With a little faith, you can say to a mountain, 'Go away!' and it will go! (Matthew 17:20)

Little Maeve saw a big mountain and said, "Mountain, go away!" She giggled and imagined it moving. A wise little bird nearby said, "With faith, you can do big things!" Maeve smiled, knowing that even a tiny bit of faith can do amazing things. Remember, with faith in your heart, you can do anything!

Reflection:

When you see something really big, like a mountain, what is something big that you can believe in your heart to help you do amazing things?

Today's Prayer:

Dear Jesus, thank you for giving me faith, even when things seem big or hard. Help me trust you and believe that I can do wonderful things with your help.

---

15 MARCH

The Gentle Voice of God

God talks gently to us like a soft breeze. (1 Kings 19:12)

A little girl loved to listen to the birds and the wind. One day, as she sat quietly, a soft breeze touched her cheek. She smiled, knowing it was God's gentle voice, reminding her that she is loved. Just like that breeze, God speaks softly to our hearts, showing us His love always.

Reflection:

Can you think of a time when you felt the soft breeze on your face? How did it make you feel, and can you imagine that breeze was God telling you that you are loved?

Today's Prayer:

Dear God, thank you for your gentle voice that whispers to my heart like a soft breeze. Help me always to listen, knowing you love me and are with me every day.

16
MARCH

Living with Kingdom Vision
Shine your light and let others see your good hearts (Matthew 5:16)

In a bright, colorful garden, there lived a little girl named Anna. Anna loved to share and be kind, just like the beautiful flowers. One sunny day, she helped a tiny bird find its way home. The . bird chirped, "Thank you, Anna! You shine like a bright star!" Anna smiled, knowing her kindness made the world brighter. Just like Anna, you can shine your light too!

Reflection:

What is something nice you can do today to help someone, just like Anna helped the little bird?

Today's Prayer:

Dear God, thank you for helping me shine my light with kindness and love. Please show me ways to help others and make the world a brighter place.

•

17
MARCH

Standing Firm in Faith
Trust in God, He is always with you!
(Isaiah 41:10)

Jade saw a strong tree standing tall in the wind. She thought, "Wow! That tree trusts the ground to hold it." Just like the tree, we can trust in God. When we feel wobbly or scared, we can remember: "Trust in God, He is always with you!" Let's be like the tree, strong and brave, knowing God's love is right beside us!

Reflection:
What do you think makes you feel strong and brave, just like the tall tree? Can you think of a time when you felt God was with you, helping you stand tall?

Today's Prayer:

Dear God, thank you for helping me stand strong and brave, just like a tall tree. Please help me trust you and remember you are always with me, no matter what.

18
MARCH

Letting Go of Shame

You are special and loved, just as you are!
(Psalm 139:14)

A shy little fox peeked from behind the trees, wishing she could be as bold as the others. One night, she heard a gentle whisper, "You are special and loved, just as you are!" The fox took a deep breath and stepped into the moonlight, her fur glowing softly. She didn't need to hide—she could shine by being herself! Sweet one, you are special too! Shine bright, knowing you are deeply loved!

Reflection:

Can you think of a time when you felt a little shy like the little fox? What makes you feel brave to shine like her?

Today's Prayer:

Dear God, thank you for loving me just as I am and making me special. Please help me feel brave to shine and be myself, even when I feel shy.

19
MARCH

Anchored in His Word

God's Word is like a big hug that keeps us safe and happy. (Psalm 119:105)

A little girl loved reading her special storybook, filled with God's words. One day, she realized those words felt like a big, warm hug! Whenever she felt scared or lost, she opened her book, and her heart lit up. Like a cozy blanket, God's Word kept her safe and happy—her very own hug from Him!

Reflection:

Can you show me how you feel safe and happy when you hear God's words, just like the little girl felt when she read her special storybook?

Today's Prayer:

Dear God, thank you for your special words that make me feel safe and loved. Please help me remember your words are always with me, like a warm hug in my heart.

20 MARCH

Brave in the Small Things
Be brave and strong, little one! God is with you always! (Psalm 27:14)

A tiny butterfly peeked out from her cozy cocoon. She wanted to fly but felt shy. Then, a gentle whisper said, "Be brave, little one! I am always with you." She took a deep breath, fluttered her wings, and leaped! Up she went, dancing among the flowers. Just like the butterfly, you can be brave in the small things, knowing God is always beside you!

Reflection:

Can you show me how you try something new or brave, even if it feels small, just like the butterfly did when she learned to fly?

Today's Prayer:

Dear God, thank you for being with me when I try new or brave things. Please help me remember you are always beside me, giving me courage in every little step.

21 MARCH

Your Pain Has a Purpose
God helps us feel better when we're sad, and He loves us always! (Psalm 147:3)

Clara sat on the grass, holding her scraped knee. Tears filled her eyes until she remembered—God loves her always! She took a deep breath and whispered a prayer. A warm feeling, like a big hug, filled her heart. Her knee still hurt a little, but she wasn't alone. Just like Clara, when you feel sad, remember—God is always with you, making your heart happy again!

Reflection:

When you're feeling sad or hurt, what is something that makes you feel happy inside, just like Clara felt God's love?

Today's Prayer:

Dear God, thank you for loving me and helping my heart feel better when I am sad or hurt. Please remind me that you are always with me, bringing comfort and happiness to my heart.

22 MARCH

A God Who Redeems
God loves you and makes everything better!
(Isaiah 43:1)

A little girl felt scared and alone. But then she remembered—God loves her! His love felt like a warm hug from her favorite blanket. She took a deep breath and sang her favorite song, feeling better inside. When you're sad or afraid, remember: God is with you and makes everything bright again!

Reflection:

When you feel scared or lonely, what is something you can do to remember that God loves you like a warm hug?

Today's Prayer:

Dear God, thank you for loving me and making everything better when I feel scared or alone. Please help me remember your love is always with me, bringing light and comfort to my heart.

---

23 MARCH

Becoming Spiritually Resilient
God's love makes me strong and gives me courage!
(Psalm 27:1)

Little Stella was inside her cozy house, watching the storm outside. The wind howled, and the rain poured, making her feel scared. But then she remembered something special—God's love makes her strong! Stella took a deep breath, held her hands tight, and whispered, "God loves me, so I'm brave!" When the storm passed, she felt peaceful and strong. Just like Stella, you can be brave too, knowing God's love will help you shine!

Reflection:

Can you show me how you feel brave and strong when you remember God loves you, just like Stella did during the storm?

Today's Prayer:

Dear God, thank you for loving me and making me strong and brave. Please help me remember your love gives me courage, even when I feel scared.

24 MARCH

Overflowing with Living Water

You can be happy like a big, flowing river because God gives us His love! (John 4:14)

Ivy played by a big, sparkling river that flowed with joy and love from God. She dipped her tiny hands in the cool water, feeling it splash all around. Giggling, she realized that God's love was like the river—always flowing and never stopping! Just like the river, we can share God's love too! Remember, sweet Ivy, you are loved!

Reflection:

Can you show me how you share God's love with others, like splashing water from a river and making everyone around you happy?

Today's Prayer:

Dear God, thank you for filling my heart with your love that never stops. Please help me share your love with others and bring happiness wherever I go.

---

25 MARCH

Choosing Rest Over Rush

God loves it when we take time to rest and be happy! (Matthew 11:28)

Lucy loved to play in the garden, but she also liked to take her time. While others rushed around, she would stop, smell the flowers, and feel the sunshine on her face. One day, the wise owl told her, "It's good to rest and feel God's love!" Lucy smiled, finding peace in the quiet. Remember, sweet one, it's okay to slow down and feel God's love with you!

Reflection:

What do you like to do when you take a little pause in the garden? Can you tell me how it feels when you stop to smell the flowers or feel the sunshine?

Today's Prayer:

Dear God, thank you for giving me quiet moments to rest and feel your love. Please help me remember to slow down and find happiness in your peaceful presence.

26 MARCH

A Heart That Seeks God

God loves you, little one, when you look for Him! (Jeremiah 29:13)

Josie loved to explore the garden, looking for the prettiest flowers. As she searched, she remembered, "God loves me when I look for Him!" So, she peeked behind the leaves, under the trees, and around the bushes. Josie found beautiful flowers and felt God's love all around her. Remember, little one, when you seek Him, you'll find His love too!

Reflection:

When you look for flowers in the garden, can you think of a way to look for God's love, too? What makes you feel happy and loved like those pretty flowers?

Today's Prayer:

Dear God, thank you for all the pretty flowers in the garden that remind me of your love. Help me always to seek you with my little heart, so I can feel your love all around me.

---

27 MARCH

Obedience in the Little Things

Even little things matter when we listen and do what's right! (Colossians 3:20)

Audrey loved to play in the sunny garden, but Mama asked her, "Can you help me pick up the little leaves?" Audrey listened and helped, even though it seemed small. When they were done, the garden sparkled! Audrey felt happy, knowing that doing little things shows love. Remember, sweet one, when we obey, we shine with joy!

Reflection:

Can you think of a time when you helped someone, like picking up leaves in the garden? How did it make you feel inside when you helped?

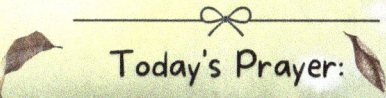

Today's Prayer:

Dear God, thank you for helping me listen and do what is right, even in little things. Please fill my heart with joy when I help others and obey.

28 MARCH

The Gift of Quiet Moments

God loves you in the quiet times.
(Psalm 46:10)

Iris loved to play all day, but sometimes, she would sit quietly with her favorite stuffed bunny. In those peaceful moments, she felt God's love, like a warm, cozy blanket. Iris learned that her heart needed quiet too, just like the flowers. Remember, sweet one, God loves you in those quiet times.

Reflection:

Can you think of a time when you sat quietly with your bunny and felt loved, just like the flowers do? What made you feel cozy and happy inside?

Today's Prayer:

Dear God, thank you for loving me in the quiet moments. Please help my heart feel cozy and happy when I sit with you and rest.

---

29 MARCH

He Carries Your Burdens

God helps us when we are sad; He carries our heavy things. Psalm 55:22

Eloise felt sad because her basket was too heavy to carry. But then, she remembered that God helps us when we feel this way! She whispered, "Please help me, God." Suddenly, Eloise felt lighter and happier. God took her worries away, helping her carry her burdens. Remember, sweet one, God is always there to help you!

Reflection:

If you ever feel like your basket is too heavy, what do you think you can say to God to help you feel better?

Today's Prayer:

Dear God, thank you for helping me when things feel too hard or heavy. Please remind me to ask for your help so my heart can feel light and happy again.

30 MARCH

Your Journey Is Sacred

God made you special, and your adventure is wonderful! (Psalm 139:14)

Joy loved to explore, running through fields and splashing in puddles. One sunny day, she picked a flower and twirled around, giggling. "God made me special, and my adventure is wonderful!" she thought. Just like Joy, you are special too! Every day is a new journey, full of fun and surprises. God is with you every step of the way!

Reflection:

Can you show me how you have fun on your own special adventure, knowing God made you unique and is with you every step?

Today's Prayer:

Dear God, thank you for making me special and being with me on all my adventures. Please help me enjoy each new day and remember you are always by my side.

---

31 MARCH

Victory in Christ

With Jesus, I can do anything!
(Philippians 4:13)

Allison wanted to climb the tallest slide at the park. She felt scared but remembered what her friend Jesus said, "With Me, you can do anything!" So, she took a deep breath and tried again. Up, up, up she went! When she slid down, she laughed with joy! Just like Allison, you can be brave too! With Jesus in your heart, you can do anything, big or small!

Reflection:

Can you show me how you try something new or brave, even if it feels a little scary, knowing Jesus is with you just like He was with Allison?

Today's Prayer:

Dear Jesus, thank you for being with me when I feel scared or try something new. Please help me be brave and remember that with you, I can do anything.

49

April

1
APRIL

Renewal in Christ

Jesus makes everything new and lovely!
(2 Corinthians 5:17)

Carla loves to draw pretty pictures and play in the garden. Sometimes, her drawings get messy or her flowers wilt, but that's okay! Jesus makes everything new and lovely again. When Carla feels sad or things go wrong, she can remember that Jesus helps her start fresh. With Jesus, every day is a new chance to smile and grow!

Reflection:

Can you show me how you start fresh and try again when something goes wrong, Knowing Jesus makes everything new and lovely, just like He does for Carla?

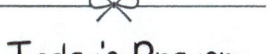

Today's Prayer:

Dear Jesus, thank you for making everything new and lovely when things go wrong. Please help me start fresh with a happy heart and trust you to help me grow and smile again.

2
APRIL

When You Need Reassurance

God loves you so much!
(1 John 4:16)

Dorothy sometimes feels unsure or a little scared, like when she tries something new. But God is always with Dorothy, holding her close and loving her so much! When Dorothy needs a hug or a gentle word, she can remember that God's love never goes away. God helps Dorothy feel brave and safe, no matter what happens each day.

Reflection:

Can you show me how you feel brave and safe when you remember God loves you and is always with you, just like Dorothy does?

Today's Prayer:

Dear God, thank you for loving me and holding me close when I feel unsure or scared. Please help me feel brave and safe, Knowing your love is always with me.

3
APRIL

Rooted in God's Word
God's Word helps me grow strong!
(Psalm 1:3)

Grace loves to water her little plant and watch it grow tall and green. Just like her plant needs water, Grace's heart needs God's Word to grow strong and happy. When Grace listens to Bible stories and learns about God, she grows inside, too! God's Word helps Grace be kind, brave, and full of love every single day.

Reflection:

What is your favorite story about God, and how do you think it can help your heart grow just like your little plant?

✄

Today's Prayer:

Dear God, thank you for your special words that help my heart grow strong and happy. Please help me listen and learn from you so I can be kind, brave, and full of love.

•

4
APRIL

Faith for the Future
God has a bright plan for you!
(Jeremiah 29:11)

Heather loves to look at the sky and dream about tomorrow. Sometimes, she wonders what she will do when she grows up. God smiles at Heather and has a bright plan just for her! Even when Heather feels unsure, she can trust God to guide her. With God's help, Heather's future is full of hope, love, and happy adventures.

Reflection:

Can you show me how you dream about tomorrow and trust that God has a bright and happy plan just for you, just like Heather does?

✄

Today's Prayer:

Dear God, thank you for having a bright and happy plan for my life. Please help me trust you with my dreams and follow you with hope and joy in my heart.

5
APRIL

Choosing Joy Daily
Choose joy every day because God loves you!
(Nehemiah 8:10)

Jane wakes up and smiles, ready for a brand-new day. Sometimes things are hard, but Jane remembers she can choose joy because God loves her so much! When Jane laughs, sings, or shares a hug, her heart feels happy. Every day, Jane can choose to be joyful, knowing God is always with her, filling her life with love.

Reflection:

Can you think of a time when you were really happy, like when you laughed, sang, or shared a hug? What made your heart feel full of joy?

Today's Prayer:

Dear God, thank you for this beautiful day and for your love that fills my heart. Help me to choose joy and share my smiles, knowing you are always with me!

6
APRIL

God's Presence in the Waiting
God is with you while you wait!
(Psalm 39:7)

Julia waits for her turn on the slide and sometimes feels a little wiggly inside. Waiting can be hard, but God is with Julia every moment! She can talk to God while she waits, knowing He is close and loves her. God helps Julia feel calm and patient. Even in the waiting, Julia is never alone—God is always with her.

Reflection:

Can you show me how you wait patiently and talk to God, just like Julia does when she waits for her turn on the slide?

Today's Prayer:

Dear God, thank you for being with me when I have to wait. Please help me feel calm and patient, knowing you are always close and love me so much.

7
APRIL

A Heart of Humility
Be kind and gentle to others, just like Jesus!
(Philippians 2:3)

Megan loves to play with her friends and share her toys.
Sometimes, she lets others go first or helps someone who needs
a hand. When Megan is kind and gentle, she is being just like
Jesus! God smiles when Megan puts others first. Every day,
Megan's humble heart shows God's love, making her a special
friend to everyone.

Reflection:

Can you think of a time when you shared your toys with a friend?
How did it make you feel inside when you helped someone?

Today's Prayer:

Dear God, thank you for helping me be kind and gentle like Jesus.
Please fill my heart with love so I can put others first and be a
special friend to everyone.

8
APRIL

Walking in God's Strength
God helps me be strong and brave!
(Isaiah 41:10)

Melanie sometimes feels small when she tries something new, like
climbing the big slide. But God is always with Melanie, helping her
be strong and brave! When Melanie feels scared, she can
remember that God gives her courage. With God's help, Melanie
can do hard things and try her best. God's strength makes
Melanie brave every single day!

Reflection:

When you feel a little scared, like when you're climbing the big slide,
who can help you be brave and strong?

Today's Prayer:

Dear God, thank you for being with me when I feel small and
scared. Help me to be strong and brave like you, so I can climb
big slides and do my best every day!

9
APRIL

Compassion Like Christ
Love others like Jesus loves us!
(John 15:12)

Penny loves to help her friends and share her favorite toys. When someone feels sad, Penny gives a gentle hug or a big smile. Jesus loves everyone, and Penny can show that same love, too! Every day, Penny's kind heart makes others feel happy. God is so glad when Penny loves others just like Jesus loves her.

Reflection:

When you see a friend feeling sad, what kind thing can you do to help them feel happy again, just like Jesus would?

Today's Prayer:

Dear Jesus, thank you for loving me and showing me how to care for others. Please help me share your love with my friends and make their hearts happy, just like you do.

10
APRIL

Overcoming Spiritual Burnout
God gives us strength when we feel tired!
(Isaiah 40:29)

Monica sometimes feels tired after a busy day of playing and learning. When her heart feels worn out, God is there to help her rest and feel strong again. Monica can talk to God and ask for His help anytime. God gives Monica new strength and fills her with love, so she can keep smiling and enjoying each new day.

Reflection:

Can you show me how you rest and talk to God when you feel tired, so He can help you feel strong and happy again, just like Monica?

Today's Prayer:

Dear God, thank You for helping Monica when she feels tired and worn out. Please fill her heart with Your love and strength so she can keep smiling and enjoying every day!

11 APRIL

The Hope of the Resurrection
Jesus loves us and brings us back to life!
(John 11:25)

Rachel loves to watch flowers bloom in the garden. Sometimes, flowers look sleepy, but soon they stand tall and bright again. Jesus loves Rachel and brings new life, just like the flowers! Even when things feel sad or hard, Jesus gives hope and joy. Rachel can remember that Jesus' love makes everything new and full of happy life.

Reflection:

Can you show me how you feel happy and full of hope, just like a flower standing tall, knowing that Jesus loves you and makes everything new?

Today's Prayer:

Dear Jesus, thank you for loving me and giving me hope when things feel hard. Please help my heart feel bright and new, just like a flower blooming in your love.

---

12 APRIL

Pouring Out, Being Filled
God fills our hearts with love when we share and give! (1 John 4:19)

Laura loves to share her snacks and give hugs to her friends. When Laura gives to others, her heart feels warm and happy. God fills Laura's heart with even more love every time she shares. Just like a cup that gets filled up, Laura's heart overflows with kindness. God loves when Laura gives and helps, making her heart full and bright!

Reflection:

Can you show me how you share or help a friend, and feel your heart fill up with love, just like Laura does?

Today's Prayer:

Dear God, thank You for the warm hugs and yummy snacks I can share with my friends. I feel so happy when I give, knowing my heart is filled with Your love and kindness!

13
APRIL

God's Provision Is Enough

God gives us what we need, just like a good friend! (Philippians 4:19)

Macy loves to have picnics with her friends and share yummy treats. Sometimes, she worries there won't be enough, but God always takes care of her. God gives Macy everything she needs, just like a good friend. When Macy shares and trusts God, her heart feels happy and safe. God's love and care are always enough for Macy every day.

Reflection:

Can you show me how you trust God to take care of you and share with your friends, just like Macy does at her picnic?

Today's Prayer:

Dear God, thank you for always giving me what I need and taking care of me. Please help me trust you and share with my friends, knowing your love is always enough.

14
APRIL

Women of Purpose

You are special and brave, just like a queen! (Esther 2:17)

Jenna loves to dress up and pretend she's a queen. God made Jenna special and brave, just like Queen Esther in the Bible! Even when Jenna feels small, God has a big purpose for her. She can help others, be kind, and show courage every day. God smiles when Jenna remembers she is loved and chosen for wonderful things!

Reflection:

Jenna, when you dress up like a queen, how can you be a good friend or help someone today, just like Queen Esther?

Today's Prayer:

Dear God, thank you for making me special and brave like Queen Esther. Please help me use my courage and kindness to help others and do wonderful things for you.

15 APRIL

Courage to Begin Again

God helps me try again, and I can be brave!
(Isaiah 41:10)

Ashley tries to build a tall tower, but sometimes it falls down. She feels a little sad, but God is always with her, helping her be brave and try again. When Ashley starts over, God gives her courage and a happy heart. Every day, Ashley can remember that with God's help, she can always begin again and do her best!

Reflection:

Can you show me how you try again and feel brave, even if something doesn't work the first time, just like Ashley does with her tower?

Today's Prayer:

Dear God, thank you for helping me be brave and try again when things are hard. Please give me courage and a happy heart every time I start over.

---

16 APRIL

Faithful in the Hidden Places

God sees you when you're playing and smiling, and He loves you very much! (Psalm 139:7-10)

In a quiet, secret garden, little Ciara loved to dance and sing among the flowers. Even when no one was around, God saw her joyful heart. "I love you, Ciara!" whispered the breeze. Ciara giggled, knowing God was always with her, even in hidden places. God sees your smiles and loves you deeply!

Reflection:

Can you show me how you feel happy and loved, even when you're by yourself, knowing God sees you and loves you just like He does with Ciara?

Today's Prayer:

Dear God, thank you for seeing me in my secret garden where I dance and sing. I'm so glad You love me always, even when I'm playing by myself.

17 APRIL

Living Light in a Heavy World

Shine your light, little one, and make the world bright! (Matthew 5:16)

Briana loves to smile and laugh, making everyone around her feel happy. Sometimes, the world feels big and heavy, but Briana can shine her light by being kind and loving. God made Briana to bring joy and hope to others. Every day, Briana's bright heart helps make the world a happier place, just like Jesus wants her to do!

Reflection:

Can you show me how you shine your light and make others happy, just like Briana does with her smiles and kindness?

———— ✣ ————

Today's Prayer:

Dear Jesus, thank you for making my heart bright and full of joy. Please help me share my smiles and kindness to make the world a happier place for everyone.

———————————— ● ————————————

18 APRIL

Trusting God with the Unknown

God loves you and will help you, even when you can't see, just like the stars shine in the night! (Psalm 56:3)

Rosie loves to look at the stars twinkling in the night sky. Sometimes, she feels unsure about what will happen next. But even when Rosie can't see everything, God is with her, loving and helping her. Just like the stars shine in the dark, God's love is always there. Rosie can trust God to guide her every day.

Reflection:

Can you show me how you trust God to help you when you feel unsure or can't see what's next, just like Rosie does when she looks at the stars?

———— ✣ ————

Today's Prayer:

Dear God, thank you for loving me and guiding me, even when I feel unsure. Please help me trust you to lead me, just like the stars shine and show the way in the night.

19 APRIL

Embracing God's Refining
God is like a warm hug, helping me grow and shine! (Isaiah 48:10)

Kimberly loves to learn new things and try her best. Sometimes, learning feels hard, but God is always with her, like a warm hug. God helps Kimberly grow and shine, even when things are tough. Every day, God's love makes Kimberly stronger and brighter. She can remember that God is helping her become the wonderful girl He made her to be!

Reflection:

Can you show me how you keep trying and learning, even when it feels hard, knowing God is helping you grow and shine, just like Kimberly?

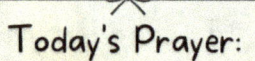

Today's Prayer:

Dear God, thank you for helping me grow and shine, even when things are hard. Please stay close to me and give me courage to keep trying, knowing your love makes me strong.

---

20 APRIL

Gratitude in the Grind
Thank you, God, for big and small things! (1 Thessalonians 5:18)

Marisol loves to play, learn, and help at home. Sometimes, her days feel busy and full, but Marisol remembers to say, "Thank you, God!" for every little thing. God loves when Marisol is thankful for her toys, her food, and her family. Every day, Marisol's grateful heart makes God smile and helps her feel happy inside, no matter what!

Reflection:

What is something fun you did today that made you want to say "Thank you, God!"?

Today's Prayer:

Dear God, thank you for all the good things you give me, big and small. Please help me remember to say thank you and keep a happy heart every day.

21
APRIL

Holding On to Hope

God loves you and is always with you, so you can be happy and hope for good things! (Psalm 31:24)

Hope loves to look for rainbows after the rain. Sometimes, she feels sad or has to wait for something special. But God is always with Hope, loving her and helping her feel happy inside. Even on hard days, Hope can trust that good things are coming. With God by her side, Hope's heart is full of joy and hope!

Reflection:

Can you show me how you look for something happy, like a rainbow, even when you feel sad or have to wait, just like Hope does?

Today's Prayer:

Dear God, thank you for being with me and filling my heart with hope, even when I feel sad or have to wait. Please help me look for your happy surprises and trust that good things are coming.

22
APRIL

The Beauty of Forgiveness

Forgiving makes our hearts happy!
(Ephesians 4:32)

Keira sometimes feels upset when someone breaks her toy or makes her sad. But when Keira chooses to forgive, her heart feels light and happy again. God loves it when Keira forgives, just like Jesus forgives us. Every day, Keira can show love by letting go of hurt. Forgiving makes Keira's heart shine bright and brings smiles to everyone!

Reflection:

Can you show me how you let go of hurt and forgive someone, so your heart can feel happy and bright, just like Keira?

Today's Prayer:

Dear Jesus, thank you for forgiving me and helping me forgive others. Please fill my heart with love so I can let go of hurt and share your happiness with everyone.

23 APRIL

God's Still Small Voice

God speaks gently to us, like a soft whisper in our hearts. (1 Kings 19:12)

Alessia loves to listen to gentle sounds, like the wind in the trees or a soft lullaby. Sometimes, when Alessia is quiet, she can feel God's love in her heart, like a tiny whisper. God speaks gently to Alessia, helping her feel safe and loved. Every day, Alessia can listen for God's soft voice guiding her with kindness.

Reflection:

Can you show me how you listen quietly for God's gentle voice, just like Alessia does when she hears the wind or a lullaby?

***

Today's Prayer:

Dear God, thank you for speaking to me with your gentle voice and filling my heart with love. Please help me listen quietly and feel safe, knowing you are always near.

•

24 APRIL

When You Feel Spiritually Empty

God loves you very much and wants to fill your heart with happiness! (Psalm 147:3)

Amie sometimes feels quiet or a little empty inside, like her favorite cup with no juice. But God loves Amie very much and wants to fill her heart with happiness! When Amie feels sad or lonely, she can talk to God, and He will help her feel better. God's love fills Amie's heart, making her feel joyful and full again.

Reflection:

Can you show me how you talk to God when you feel a little sad or empty, and let Him fill your heart with happiness, just like Amie does?

***

Today's Prayer:

Dear God, thank you for loving me and wanting to fill my heart with happiness. Please help me talk to you when I feel sad or lonely, so your love can make me joyful and full again.

25 APRIL

Peace That Transcends
Jesus gives us peace that makes us happy!
(John 14:27)

Maya loves to sit quietly and watch the clouds float by. Sometimes, things around her feel busy or noisy, but Jesus gives Maya a special peace inside her heart. When Maya feels calm and happy, she knows Jesus is with her. Every day, Maya can remember that Jesus' peace helps her feel safe, loved, and full of joy.

Reflection:

When you sit quietly and watch the clouds, how does your heart feel when you remember that Jesus is with you?

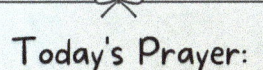

Today's Prayer:

Dear Jesus, thank you for giving me your special peace that makes my heart feel calm and happy. Please help me remember you are always with me, bringing love and joy wherever I go.

---

26 APRIL

Carrying God's Light
Shine your light, so everyone can see
God's love! (Matthew 5:16)

Alora loves to smile and help her friends. When she is kind and shares, she shines her light for everyone to see. God made Alora special, and her bright heart shows God's love to the world. Every day, Alora can carry God's light by being loving and helpful, making everyone around her feel happy and cared for.

Reflection:

Can you think of a time today when you made someone smile? How did it feel to share your light with them?

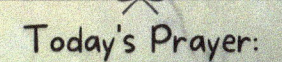

Today's Prayer:

Dear God, thank you for making me special and giving me your light to share. Please help me be loving and helpful, so I can make others feel happy and show your love to the world.

27 APRIL

Standing on God's Promises

God keeps His promises,
and we can trust Him! (Psalm 145:13)

Blaire loves to build tall towers with her blocks. Sometimes, they fall down, but God's promises never do! God always keeps His promises, and Blaire can trust Him every day. When Blaire feels worried or unsure, she remembers that God is always with her. Standing on God's promises helps Blaire feel safe, strong, and full of hope.

Reflection:

Can you show me how you trust God and feel hopeful, even when things don't go as planned, just like Blaire does when her towers fall down?

Today's Prayer:

Dear God, thank you for keeping your promises and being with me when things are hard. Please help me trust you and feel hopeful, even when things don't go the way I want.

---

28 APRIL

Finding Rest in His Love

God loves you so much, and in His love,
you can rest happy! (1 John 4:16)

Lacey loves to snuggle with her soft blanket and listen to gentle songs. Sometimes, she feels tired or needs a quiet moment. God loves Lacey so much, and His love is like a cozy hug. When Lacey rests in God's love, her heart feels happy and safe. Every day, Lacey can find peace and comfort in God's loving arms.

Reflection:

Can you show me how you feel cozy and safe when you rest in God's love, just like Lacey does with her soft blanket?

Today's Prayer:

Dear God, thank you for loving me and giving me a safe place to rest. Please help my heart feel cozy and happy in your love, just like when I snuggle with my blanket.

29
APRIL

Walking by Faith, Not Sight

God is with you, little one, even when you
can't see Him! (2 Corinthians 5:7)

Carol loves to play hide and seek, sometimes not seeing her
friends right away. Even when she can't see them, she knows
they're there. God is just like that! Carol can't always see God,
but He is always with her, loving and guiding her. Every day,
Carol can trust God and walk by faith, knowing He's close by.

Reflection:

Can you show me how you trust God is with you, even
when you can't see Him, just like Carol does when she
plays hide and seek?

Today's Prayer:

Dear God, thank you for being with me even when I can't see
you. Please help me trust your love and know you are always
close, guiding me every day.

30
APRIL

God's Grace Through Every Season

God loves you always, in every season!
(Psalm 100:5)

Violet loves to jump in puddles in spring, pick flowers in summer,
and watch leaves fall in autumn. In every season, God loves
Violet so much! When it's sunny or rainy, warm or cold, God's
grace is always with her. Violet can smile and feel safe, knowing
God's love never changes, no matter what season she is in.

Reflection:

Can you show me how you feel happy and safe in every season,
knowing God loves you always, just like Violet does?

Today's Prayer:

Dear God, thank you for loving me in every season, whether it's
sunny, rainy, warm, or cold. Please help me feel safe and happy,
knowing your love is always with me.

May

1 MAY

Grace for Today

God loves you every day!
(Romans 5:8)

Quinn wakes up each day ready to play and learn new things. Sometimes, she makes mistakes or feels a little sad. But God loves Quinn every single day, no matter what! God's grace means He forgives and helps her try again. Every day, Quinn can smile and remember that God's love is always with her, making her heart happy.

Reflection:

Can you show me how you smile and try again when you make a mistake, knowing God loves you every day, just like Quinn?

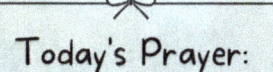

Today's Prayer:

Dear God, thank you for loving me every day, even when I make mistakes. Please help me smile, try again, and remember your love is always with me.

2 MAY

Becoming a Prayerful Woman

God loves to hear our prayers!
(1 Thessalonians 5:17)

Alyssa loves to talk to God, telling Him about her day and her friends. God loves to hear Alyssa's prayers, no matter how big or small. When Alyssa prays, she feels close to God and knows He is listening. Every day, Alyssa can talk to God about anything, and His love fills her heart with peace and joy.

Reflection:

Can you think of a special thing you want to tell God about your day that makes you happy?

Today's Prayer:

Dear God, thank you for listening to me when I talk to you about my day. Please fill my heart with your love and help me remember I can pray to you anytime.

67

3 MAY

God's Strength in Your Story

God is my helper; I am not afraid!
(Psalm 118:6)

Jada loves to try new things, but sometimes she feels a little scared. When Jada remembers that God is her helper, she feels brave inside! God is always with Jada, giving her strength for every part of her story. Every day, Jada can trust God to help her, so she doesn't have to be afraid of anything.

Reflection:

Can you show me how you trust God to help you be brave when you try something new, just like Jada does?

Today's Prayer:

Dear God, thank you for being my helper and giving me strength when I feel scared. Please help me be brave and trust you whenever I try something new.

---

4 MAY

Restoring Your Soul

God helps us feel better and happy inside.
(Psalm 23:3)

Megan sometimes feels tired or a little sad after a busy day. But God is always there to help her feel better and happy inside. When Megan talks to God or listens to gentle songs, her heart feels calm and peaceful. Every day, God's love restores Megan's soul, giving her new joy and helping her feel strong again.

Reflection:

Can you show me how you let God help your heart feel better and happy, just like Megan does when she talks to Him or listens to gentle songs?

Today's Prayer:

Dear God, thank you for helping my heart feel better and happy when I am tired or sad. Please fill me with your love and peace so I can feel strong and joyful again.

5 MAY

Trusting God in the Unknown

God is with you everywhere you go
(Joshua 1:9)

Brittany loves to explore new places and try new things. Sometimes, she feels a little nervous when she doesn't know what will happen next. But God is always with Brittany, no matter where she goes! She can trust God to guide her and keep her safe. Every day, Brittany can remember that God's love goes with her everywhere.

Reflection:

Can you show me how you feel brave and trust God to be with you when you go somewhere new, just like Brittany does?

Today's Prayer:

Dear God, thank you for being with me wherever I go and helping me feel brave. Please guide me and keep me safe when I try new things or visit new places.

---

6 MAY

Overflowing with Compassion

Love others like a big hug from your heart!
(1 John 4:7)

Leanna loves to give big hugs and help her friends when they need it. When Leanna shares her toys or says kind words, her heart feels warm and happy. God loves when Leanna shows compassion, just like a big hug from her heart! Every day, Leanna can make the world brighter by loving others the way God loves her.

Reflection:

Can you show me how you give a big hug or help a friend, sharing love from your heart just like Leanna does?

Today's Prayer:

Dear God, thank you for filling my heart with love and compassion. Please help me share big hugs and kind words, making the world brighter for my friends and family.

7 MAY

The Power of a Grateful Heart

Be thankful and happy, for God loves you!
(1 Thessalonians 5:18)

Aliya loves to say "thank you" for her toys, her food, and her family. When Aliya is thankful, her heart feels happy and full of joy. God loves it when Aliya has a grateful heart! Every day, Aliya can remember to thank God for all the good things. Being thankful helps Aliya feel close to God and share happiness with others.

Reflection:

Can you show me how you say "thank you" for something special, just like Aliya does, and feel your heart fill up with joy?

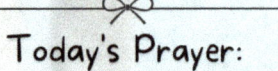

Today's Prayer:

Dear God, thank you for all the good things you give me and for loving me so much. Please help me have a thankful heart and share my joy with others every day.

---

8 MAY

Faith in the Storm

Jesus is with us in the storm,
and we are safe in His love! (Mark 4:39)

Valerie sometimes hears thunder or sees rain falling outside and feels a little scared. But Jesus is always with Valerie, even in the storm! When Valerie remembers Jesus' love, her heart feels safe and calm. Every day, Valerie can trust that Jesus will take care of her, no matter what. With Jesus, Valerie is never alone, even in stormy times.

Reflection:

Can you show me how you trust Jesus to keep you safe and feel calm inside, even when you hear thunder or see rain, just like Valerie does?

Today's Prayer:

Dear Jesus, thank you for staying with me and keeping me safe when I feel scared in the storm. Please help my heart feel calm and peaceful, knowing your love is always with me.

9 MAY

When You Feel Invisible

You are special and God loves you very much!
(Jeremiah 31:3)

Katelyn sometimes feels small or left out when others don't notice her. But God always sees Katelyn and loves her very much! She is special to God, even when she feels invisible. Every day, Katelyn can remember that God's love is always with her. God made Katelyn unique and precious, and she is never alone in His care.

Reflection:

Can you show me how you feel special and loved, even when you feel small or left out, Knowing God always sees you just like He sees Katelyn?

Today's Prayer:

Dear God, thank you for always seeing me and loving me, even when I feel small or left out. Please help me remember I am special and never alone in your care.

---

10 MAY

Rooted in God's Love

God loves you so much!
(1 John 4:16)

Evangeline loves to watch flowers grow in the garden. Their roots go deep into the ground to stay strong. God's love is like those roots—always holding Evangeline safe and close. Even when she feels small, God's love helps her grow big and brave. Every day, Evangeline can remember she is rooted in God's love, and He is always with her.

Reflection:

Can you show me how you feel strong and safe, Knowing God's love holds you close and helps you grow, just like the flowers in the garden?

Today's Prayer:

Dear God, thank you for loving me and helping me grow strong, just like the flowers in the garden. Please help me feel safe and brave, Knowing your love is always holding me close.

A Quiet Spirit, A Powerful Faith

11 MAY

God loves when we are kind and calm inside.
(1 Peter 3:4)

Joanne loves to sit quietly and listen to gentle sounds, like birds singing or the wind in the trees. When Joanne is calm and kind, her heart feels peaceful and happy. God loves when Joanne has a quiet spirit and trusts Him. Every day, Joanne's gentle heart shows her strong faith, and God fills her with love and joy.

Reflection:

Can you show me how you sit quietly and listen to gentle sounds, feeling peaceful and happy inside, just like Joanne does?

Today's Prayer:

Dear God, thank you for filling my heart with peace and joy when I am quiet and calm. Please help me trust you and show kindness, so my spirit can be gentle and full of your love.

Mothering with Grace

12 MAY

Her smile is like sunshine, making everyone happy! (Proverbs 15:13)

Gianna loves to care for her dolls and give them sweet hugs. Her gentle smile makes everyone feel happy, just like sunshine. God fills Gianna's heart with grace and kindness, helping her show love to others. Every day, Gianna can share her sunshine smile and caring heart, making her world brighter with God's special love and gentle grace.

Reflection:

Can you think of a time when you gave your doll a big hug and made her feel happy? How did that make you feel inside?

Today's Prayer:

Dear God, thank you for filling my heart with kindness and grace. Please help me share my sunshine smile and gentle hugs to make others feel loved and happy.

13 MAY

Persevering in Prayer

Always talk to God, and He will listen to you!
(1 Thessalonians 5:17)

Skylene loves to talk to God about her day, her friends, and her dreams. Sometimes, she has to wait for answers, but God always listens. When Skylene keeps praying, her heart feels strong and hopeful. Every day, Skylene can remember that God loves to hear her prayers and will help her, no matter how long she waits or what she needs.

Reflection:

Can you show me how you keep talking to God and feel hopeful in your heart, even when you have to wait for answers, just like Skylene does?

Today's Prayer:

Dear God, thank you for always listening to me when I pray. Please help me keep talking to you and trust that you will help me, even when I have to wait.

---

14 MAY

The Lord Is Your Shepherd

The Lord is your shepherd, He takes care of you!" (Psalm 23:1)

Marianne loves to pretend she's a little lamb in a green field. Just like a shepherd cares for his sheep, God takes care of Marianne every day. When she feels lost or scared, God is always close, guiding and loving her. Marianne can trust that the Lord is her shepherd, keeping her safe and happy wherever she goes.

Reflection:

Can you show me how you trust God to take care of you and feel safe, just like a little lamb with her shepherd?

Today's Prayer:

Dear God, thank you for being my shepherd and taking care of me every day. Please help me feel safe and happy, knowing you are always close and loving me.

15 MAY

Letting Go of Bitterness
Let go and be happy, just like Jesus loves us!
(Ephesians 4:31-32)

Emmy sometimes feels upset when someone is unkind or takes her toy. But when Emmy lets go of her hurt and forgives, her heart feels light and happy again. Jesus loves Emmy and helps her let go of bitterness. Every day, Emmy can choose to forgive, just like Jesus, and her heart will be filled with joy and love.

Reflection:

Can you show me how you let go of hurt and forgive someone, so your heart can feel light and happy again, just like Emmy?

Today's Prayer:

Dear Jesus, thank you for helping me let go of hurt and forgive others. Please fill my heart with your joy and love so I can be happy and kind, just like you.

---

16 MAY

Walking in Spiritual Freedom
You are free to dance and play
because Jesus loves you! (Galatians 5:1)

Ainsley loves to dance, run, and play in the sunshine. Jesus gives Ainsley a happy heart and makes her free! She doesn't have to worry or feel afraid because Jesus loves her so much. Every day, Ainsley can enjoy her freedom, knowing God is with her. With Jesus, Ainsley is free to laugh, play, and be herself!

Reflection:

When you dance and play in the sunshine, how does it make your heart feel knowing that Jesus loves you and makes you free?

Today's Prayer:

Dear Jesus, thank you for loving me and giving me a happy, free heart. Please help me enjoy every moment and remember I can always be myself with you by my side.

17
MAY

Your Story Isn't Over
God has good things waiting for you!
(Jeremiah 29:11)

Edith loves to read stories and imagine happy endings. Sometimes, she feels sad when things don't go her way. But God has good things waiting for Edith, and her story isn't over! Every day is a new page with God's love and hope. Edith can trust that God is writing a beautiful story just for her, full of joy.

Reflection:

What is your favorite happy ending from a story, and what do you think will happen next in your story with God?

Today's Prayer:

Dear God, thank you for writing a beautiful story for me and filling my life with hope. Please help me trust you with every new day and look forward to all the good things you have planned for me.

18
MAY

Strength to Forgive
God helps us be kind and forgive others.
(Ephesians 4:32)

Mikayla sometimes feels hurt when someone takes her toy or says unkind words. But God helps Mikayla be kind and forgive others, just like Jesus does. When Mikayla forgives, her heart feels light and happy again. Every day, Mikayla can ask God for strength to forgive, knowing that God's love helps her be gentle, kind, and full of joy.

Reflection:

Can you show me how you ask God to help you forgive someone, so your heart can feel gentle and happy, just like Mikayla?

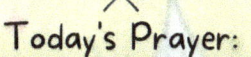

Today's Prayer:

Dear God, thank you for helping me be kind and forgive others when I feel hurt. Please give me your strength so my heart can be gentle, happy, and full of your love.

19 MAY

Faithful Through the Seasons

God loves you every day,
like the sun and the rain! (Psalm 136:1)

Sienna loves to splash in puddles when it rains and play outside when the sun is shining. No matter what the weather is, God loves Sienna every single day! God's love is always there, like the sun and the rain. Sienna can remember that God is faithful through every season, Keeping her safe, happy, and loved all the time.

Reflection:

Can you show me how you feel happy and loved, whether it's sunny or rainy, Knowing God is always with you just like He is with Sienna?

Today's Prayer:

Dear God, thank you for loving me in every season, whether it's sunny or rainy. Please help me feel safe and happy, Knowing your love is always with me no matter what.

---

20 MAY

Chosen and Cherished

You are special and loved
just like a shiny star! (Isaiah 43:4)

Layla loves to look at the stars twinkling in the night sky. God made Layla special and loves her so much—just like a shiny star! Even when Layla feels small, she is chosen and cherished by God. Every day, Layla can remember that she is precious to God, shining bright with His love wherever she goes.

Reflection:

Can you show me how you shine bright and feel special, Knowing God loves you and made you just like a shiny star, just like Layla?

Today's Prayer:

Dear God, thank you for making me special and loving me so much. Please help me shine bright with your love and remember I am always your precious child.

21 MAY

God's Peace in Pressure

God gives us peace in our hearts, even when we feel busy or scared. (Philippians 4:7)

Julianna sometimes feels busy with lots to do or a little scared when things are hard. But God gives Julianna peace in her heart, like a gentle hug. When Julianna stops and talks to God, she feels calm and safe. Every day, God's peace helps Julianna handle anything, reminding her that she is loved and never alone, no matter what.

Reflection:

When you feel busy or a little scared, what is something you can tell God to help you feel calm and loved, just like a gentle hug?

Today's Prayer:

Dear God, thank you for giving me peace in my heart when I feel busy or scared. Please help me remember to talk to you so I can feel calm, safe, and loved every day.

22 MAY

A Life That Bears Fruit

Being kind and loving is like a beautiful tree that grows good fruit! (John 15:5)

Sophia loves to help her friends and share her toys. When Sophia is kind and loving, it's like she's a beautiful tree growing sweet fruit! God is so happy when Sophia's heart is full of love. Every day, Sophia can show kindness and care, knowing that her loving actions help her grow strong and make the world a happier place.

Reflection:

Can you show me how you share or help a friend, growing good fruit in your heart just like Sophia does when she is kind and loving?

Today's Prayer:

Dear God, thank you for helping me grow good fruit in my heart when I am kind and loving. Please help me share and care for others so I can make the world a happier place.

77

23 MAY

Unshakeable Faith
*God loves you always,
and you can trust Him! (Psalm 13:5)*

Bella loves to build tall towers with her blocks. Sometimes, they fall down, but God's love never does! Even when things go wrong, Bella can trust God to help her. God loves Bella always, no matter what. Every day, Bella's faith grows strong when she remembers that God is with her, holding her close and keeping her safe.

Reflection:

Can you show me how you trust God and feel safe, even when things go wrong, just like Bella does when her towers fall down?

Today's Prayer:

Dear God, thank you for loving me and keeping me safe, even when things go wrong. Please help me trust you and remember you are always holding me close.

---

24 MAY

Celebrating Small Victories
*Every little step is special and brings us joy!
(Psalm 118:24)*

Kaia loves to try new things, like tying her shoes or drawing a picture. Every little step she takes is special and makes God smile! When Kaia celebrates her small victories, her heart fills with joy. God is happy for Kaia's big and small wins. Every day, Kaia can remember that God loves every step she takes.

Reflection:

Can you show me how you celebrate something new you learned or did today, just like Kaia does, knowing God is happy for every little step you take?

Today's Prayer:

Dear God, thank you for being happy with every little step I take. Please help me celebrate my small victories and remember that you love and cheer for me always.

25
MAY

Serving with a Joyful Heart
Serve others with a happy heart!
(Psalm 100:2)

Zara loves to help her family by picking up toys and sharing with her friends. When Zara serves others with a happy heart, she makes God smile! God loves when Zara is cheerful and kind while helping. Every day, Zara can remember that serving others is a special way to show God's love and fill her own heart with joy.

Reflection:

Can you show me how you help someone or share with a happy heart, just like Zara does when she serves her family and friends?

---✂---

Today's Prayer:

Dear God, thank you for giving me ways to help and share with others. Please fill my heart with joy so I can serve my family and friends with a big, happy smile.

26
MAY

When God Redirects Your Path
God helps me find the way
when I feel lost. (Proverbs 3:5-6)

Georgia loves to explore new places, but sometimes she feels lost or unsure which way to go. God is always with Georgia, helping her find the right path. When Georgia listens to God and trusts Him, He gently guides her steps. Every day, Georgia can remember that God's love will always help her find her way, no matter what.

Reflection:

Can you show me how you listen and trust God to help you find your way, just like Georgia does when she feels lost or unsure?

---✂---

Today's Prayer:

Dear God, thank you for guiding me when I feel lost or don't know which way to go. Please help me listen to you and trust your love to lead me on the right path.

27 MAY

Healed and Whole in Christ
Jesus makes us all better and happy!
(John 10:10)

Lani loves to swing high at the playground, feeling the wind and sunshine. When she swings, her heart feels happy and free! Sometimes, Lani feels sad or gets a little hurt, but Jesus is always with her. Jesus helps Lani feel better and whole again, filling her with joy so she can smile and swing every day.

Reflection:

Can you show me how you feel happy and free, Knowing Jesus is with you and helps you feel better, just like Lani does when she swings?

Today's Prayer:

Dear Jesus, thank you for being with me and helping me feel happy and free. Please fill my heart with your joy and help me smile, even when I feel sad or hurt.

---

28 MAY

The Joy of Obedience
Listening brings happiness!
(Proverbs 1:5)

Gemma loves to listen to her parents and teachers. When she follows their words, her heart feels happy and light! God is glad when Gemma listens and obeys, just like Jesus did. Every day, Gemma can remember that listening brings joy and helps her grow. Obeying with a happy heart makes Gemma shine with God's love and Kindness.

Reflection:

Can you show me how you listen and obey with a happy heart, just like Gemma does, and feel God's love shining in you?

Today's Prayer:

Dear God, thank you for helping me listen and obey with a happy heart. Please fill me with your love and Kindness so I can shine bright for you every day.

29 MAY

Courage to Trust Again

Be strong and brave; trust in God who loves you!" (Psalm 27:14)

Esme sometimes feels scared to try again when something goes wrong. But God loves Esme and helps her be strong and brave! When Esme trusts God, her heart feels safe and happy. Every day, Esme can remember that God is always with her, giving her courage to trust again and try new things, Knowing she is never alone.

Reflection:

Can you show me how you feel brave and try again, trusting God to help you, just like Esme does when something goes wrong?

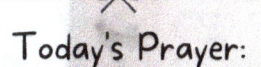

Today's Prayer:

Dear God, thank you for loving me and helping me be brave when things go wrong. Please give me courage to trust you and try again, Knowing I am never alone.

---

30 MAY

Restoring What Was Lost

God helps us find what we lose, just like he brings back happy things! (Psalm 23:3)

Shelby sometimes loses her favorite toy or feels sad when something is missing. But God is always with Shelby, helping her find what was lost and bringing back happy things. When Shelby asks God for help, He listens and cares for her. Every day, Shelby can trust that God's love will restore her joy and make her heart happy again.

Reflection:

Can you show me how you ask God for help when you lose something or feel sad, and trust Him to bring back your joy, just like Shelby does?

Today's Prayer:

Dear God, thank you for caring about me when I feel sad or lose something special. Please help me trust you to bring back my joy and fill my heart with happiness again.

Finishing the Month Faithfully
You are a light that shines bright!
(Matthew 5:14)

Zahra loves to finish her puzzles and color all the pages in her book. At the end of the month, Zahra can look back and see how much she has grown and learned! Sometimes, finishing something can feel hard, but God is always with Zahra, helping her every step of the way. God made Zahra to shine bright, just like a light in the world. When Zahra is faithful and keeps trying, she makes God smile. Every day, Zahra's kindness, joy, and hard work help her finish strong. God's love shines through Zahra, and she can share His light with everyone around her, making the world a happier place.

Reflection:

Can you show me how you keep trying and finish what you start, even when it feels hard, knowing God is helping you shine bright just like Zahra?

Today's Prayer:

Dear God, thank you for helping me keep going and finish what I start, even when it's hard. Please help me shine your light and share your love with everyone around me.

June

1
JUNE

Faith That Perseveres
Keep trusting God, for He is always with you! (Isaiah 41:10)

Callie wanted to jump high on the swings, but sometimes she felt scared. She remembered, "God is with me!" With each try, she swung higher, smiling big. Even when it was hard, Callie kept trusting God. Just like Callie, when things feel tough, remember: God is with you, helping you grow strong and brave!

Reflection:

Can you show me how you keep trying and trust God to help you be strong and brave, just like Callie does on the swings?

Today's Prayer:

Dear God, thank you for being with me and helping me be strong and brave when things are hard. Please help me keep trusting you and never give up, just like Callie.

2
JUNE

God's Timing Is Always Right
God knows when it's the right time for everything, just like the sunshine comes at the perfect time!
(Ecclesiastes 3:1)

Joyce wanted to grow tall and strong, but sometimes she felt like she had to wait. One day, she remembered that God knows the perfect time for everything. Just like the sun warms the flowers, God has a special plan for her. When the time is right, Joyce will bloom just beautifully! Trust in God's timing!

Reflection:

Can you show me how you wait patiently and trust God's timing, just like Joyce does when she waits to grow and bloom?

Today's Prayer:

Dear God, thank you for having a special plan for me and knowing the perfect time for everything. Please help me wait patiently and trust you, just like Joyce waits to grow and bloom.

84

3
JUNE

Living with Open Hands
"God loves it when we share and help others!
(Acts 20:35)

Cora had a basket full of shiny apples and saw a bunny who was sad and hungry. "I can share!" she thought. Cora gave the bunny an apple, and the bunny's eyes sparkled with joy! Cora felt so happy inside. Sharing with others makes our hearts bright, just like the sun on a happy day!

Reflection:

If you had a basket full of shiny apples, who would you share them with to make their heart feel bright?

Today's Prayer:

Dear God, thank you for the shiny apples and for helping us share. Please help us be kind like Cora, and make others happy when we give and help.

4
JUNE

The Power of God's Word
God's words are like a light that helps us see!
(Psalm 119:105)

Stefie loved to play in the garden, but sometimes it got dark, and she couldn't see where to go. Then, she remembered God's special words: "God's words are like a light!" Stefie whispered those words, and bright light filled the garden! She danced happily, knowing God's words always guide her, keeping her safe!

Reflection:

Can you show me how you feel safe and happy when you remember God's words, just like Stefie does when the garden gets dark?

Today's Prayer:

Dear God, thank you for your special words that guide me and help me feel safe. Please help me remember your words when I feel unsure, so I can be happy and brave like Stefie.

5 JUNE

Anchored in Hope

God loves you so much and keeps you safe like a cozy hug. (Romans 15:13)

Daniela felt wobbly like a little boat on the water, but then she remembered that God loves her like a cozy hug, keeping her safe. "I am anchored in hope!" she sang. As the gentle waves rocked her, Daniela smiled, knowing God always protects her. She felt safe, just like a warm blanket.

Reflection:

Can you show me how you feel safe and happy, knowing God holds you close and keeps you safe, just like Daniela in her little boat?

Today's Prayer:

Dear God, thank you for loving me and keeping me safe, just like a cozy hug. Please help me feel your hope and protection whenever I feel wobbly or unsure.

---

6 JUNE

Trusting God's Process

God has a special plan for you, sweet girl! (Jeremiah 29:11)

Karina loved to play and run, but sometimes she didn't understand why things took time. One day, a wise friend told her, "Trust the process, sweet girl! God has a special plan for you." Karina smiled, grew strong, and soon saw that God's plan was perfect, making her heart soar with joy!

Reflection:

Can you show me how you wait and trust that God has a special plan for you, just like Karina did when things took time?

Today's Prayer:

Dear God, thank you for having a special plan just for me. Please help me trust you and wait with a happy heart, knowing your plan is always good.

7
JUNE

Purpose in the Pain
God helps us feel better when we're sad.
(Psalm 34:18)

Alana, a little butterfly, felt sad when her wings got wet in the rain. She wanted to fly but couldn't. Remembering God, she whispered, "Help me feel better." The sun peeked out, drying her wings. Alana learned that even rainy days help her grow strong. God helps us feel better, just like the sunshine after the rain.

Reflection:

Can you show me how you trust God to help you feel better and strong, even after a sad or rainy day, just like Alana the butterfly?

Today's Prayer:

Dear God, thank you for helping me feel better and grow strong, even on sad or rainy days. Please remind me that your love is always with me, bringing sunshine to my heart.

8
JUNE

Finding Rest in Surrender
Come to me, and I will give you rest.
(Matthew 11:28)

Dana loved to run and play, but sometimes she felt so tired. One day, she heard a gentle voice say, "Come to me, and I will give you rest." Dana followed the voice to a cozy spot in the meadow. She snuggled in, feeling warm and safe. Dana learned that resting makes her happy and strong again. Just like Dana, you can find rest whenever you need it.

Reflection:

When you feel tired after playing a lot, where is your cozy spot to rest and feel safe? What makes that spot special for you?

Today's Prayer:

Dear God, thank you for giving me a cozy place to rest when I feel tired. Please help me remember to come to you for comfort and strength, so I can feel happy and safe again.

9 JUNE

Spiritual Refreshment
God gives us happy hearts, just like sunshine!
(Psalm 51:12)

Lynn loved to play outside in the sunny meadow. One day, as she danced, the warm sun whispered, "I fill your heart with happiness, just like I make the flowers bloom!" Lynn twirled with joy, feeling the sunshine make her smile. Just like Lynn, when we remember God's love, our hearts shine bright. Let's dance and sing with joy, knowing God makes us happy!

Reflection:

Can you show me how you dance or sing with joy, feeling God's love make your heart shine bright, just like Lynn in the sunny meadow?

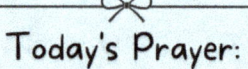

Today's Prayer:

Dear God, thank you for filling my heart with happiness and making me shine bright like the sunshine. Please help me dance and sing with joy, remembering your love every day.

---

10 JUNE

A New Song in Your Heart
God puts a happy song in our hearts!
(Psalm 40:3)

Sandra loved to play in the garden, where the flowers swayed and the sun shone bright. One day, she heard a joyful tune and sang along, feeling God's love fill her heart. Just like Sandra, God fills you with a special song that makes you smile and twirl. Whenever you feel happy, sing your song, and let the world shine with your joy!

Reflection:

Can you show me how you sing your happy song and let your heart shine with joy, just like Sandra does in the garden?

Today's Prayer:

Dear God, thank you for the beautiful flowers and the happy song in my heart. Help me to sing and twirl, sharing your love and joy with everyone around me.

Confident in His Calling

11 JUNE

God loves you and made you special!
(Psalm 139:14)

Pearl loved to play pretend, imagining she was a treasure hunter in her own backyard. One day, she found a sparkling shell and whispered, "God loves me!" Just like the shell, Pearl was special, made with love. Every adventure she had reminded her that God chose her to shine bright. You're special too, little one!

Reflection:

When you pretend to be a treasure hunter, what special things do you find that remind you how much God loves you?

Today's Prayer:

Dear God, thank you for making me special and choosing me to shine bright. Please help me remember your love on every adventure and feel confident in who you made me to be.

Healing Takes Time

12 JUNE

God is like a warm hug that helps us feel better and get well, even if it takes a little time. (Psalm 147:3)

Fatima scraped her knee while playing, and it made her feel sad. But God wrapped her in love, like a soft blanket, and whispered, "I will help you heal." Each day, her knee felt a little better, just like magic! Healing takes time, and with God's love, we get stronger and closer to joy.

Reflection:

Can you show me how you feel better and stronger each day, knowing God is helping you heal, just like Fatima with her scraped knee?

Today's Prayer:

Dear God, thank you for wrapping me in your love and helping me heal when I feel hurt or sad. Please help me be patient as I get stronger each day, trusting that your love is making me better.

89

13 JUNE — Peace When You Don't Understand

God loves you and helps you feel calm inside, even when things are confusing. (Philippians 4:7)

Nina felt a little worried when the rain started falling. She didn't understand why it was cloudy, but then she remembered, "God loves me!" Nina took a deep breath, and a warm feeling filled her heart. She sang a happy song, and soon the sun peeked out again. When things feel confusing, God helps us feel calm inside!

Reflection:

What do you like to sing or do when you feel a little worried, just like Nina did when the rain came?

Today's Prayer:

Dear God, when the skies are gray and I feel a little scared, please help me remember that Your love is always there. Fill my heart with peace and joy, just like the sunshine after the rain.

---

14 JUNE — Your Prayers Matter

God loves to hear you pray!
(1 John 5:14)

Riley loved to talk to God, just like she talked to her dolls. One sunny day, she said, "Dear God, thank You for my family and my toys!" God smiled because He loves hearing Riley's prayers. Just like Riley's whispers to her toys, our prayers matter to God. Remember, God is always listening and loves you so much!

Reflection:

Can you show me how you talk to God about the things you love, just like Riley does, and know that He is always listening to your prayers?

Today's Prayer:

Dear God, thank You for my family and my toys. I love talking to You just like I talk to my dolls, because I know You love to hear me pray!

15 JUNE

When God Feels Distant

God is always with you, even when you can't see Him! (Psalm 139:7)

Lexi felt lonely in the big, wide garden. She looked around and didn't see her friends or the bright stars. But Lexi remembered a special secret: "God is always with me, even when I can't see Him!" She closed her eyes and felt a warm hug from God. Lexi smiled, knowing He was there, watching over her. Just like Lexi, you can always trust that God is with you too!

Reflection:

Can you show me how you feel safe and loved, even when you can't see anyone around, knowing God is always with you just like He is with Lexi?

Today's Prayer:

Dear God, thank you for being with me, even when I feel alone or can't see you. Please help me feel your love and remember you are always watching over me, keeping me safe.

---

16 JUNE

His Mercy is Enough

God's love is big and always helps me—His mercy is enough! (Psalm 136:1)

Lucy loved to play in the bright, happy garden, but sometimes, she felt sad or scared. One day, she heard a gentle whisper, "Sweet Lucy, my mercy is enough! I love you so big!" Lucy smiled and twirled, knowing God's love made everything better. Just like Lucy, remember that God's love helps us, and His mercy is always there.

Reflection:

Can you show me how you feel better and smile again, knowing God's love and mercy are always there for you, just like Lucy?

Today's Prayer:

Dear God, thank You for loving me so big, just like when I play in the happy garden. When I feel sad or scared, remind me that Your mercy is enough and You always help me.

17 JUNE

Walking Boldly with God
God is with me, so I can be brave!
(Psalm 27:1)

In a sunny meadow, there lived a little girl named Ivory. Ivory wanted to explore and play, but sometimes, she felt scared. One day, she remembered, "God is with me, so I can be brave!" She took a deep breath, smiled, and took each step boldly. Just like Ivory, remember: God is with you, so you can be brave!

Reflection:

Can you show me how you take a brave step and smile, knowing God is with you just like He is with Ivory?

Today's Prayer:

Dear God, thank you for being with me and helping me be brave when I feel scared. Please help me take bold steps and smile, knowing you are always by my side.

---

18 JUNE

Less of Me, More of Him
All the good things come from God, let's share His love! *(James 1:17)*

Alisson loved to play with her toys, but one day, she noticed how happy she felt when she shared with her friends. When she shared her toys, her heart felt fuller! Alisson remembered that all good things come from God. So, she decided, "Less of me, more of Him!" She shared love and joy everywhere she went.

Reflection:

Can you show me how you share your toys or kindness with others, letting God's love fill your heart just like Alisson?

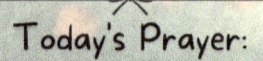

Today's Prayer:

Dear God, thank you for giving me good things to share with others. Please help me show your love and kindness, so my heart can be full of joy just like Alisson's.

19
JUNE

The Joy of Trusting
Trust in God, He loves you so!
Psalm 56:3

Matilda loved to run and play, but sometimes she felt scared. One day, she remembered a special secret: "Trust in God, He loves you so!" With a brave smile, Matilda took a big step and ran with joy. She knew God was with her, keeping her safe. Just like Matilda, you can trust God all the time!

Reflection:

Can you show me how you trust God and feel brave, even when you feel a little scared, just like Matilda does when she runs and plays?

Today's Prayer:

Dear God, thank you for loving me and helping me feel brave when I am scared. Please help me trust you and run with joy, knowing you are always with me.

20
JUNE

A Light for the World
You are a light that shines bright!
(Matthew 5:16)

Reina loved to smile and help others, just like a little light in the world. One day, she realized that when she shared and loved, her heart shone bright. Every time she smiled, she made the world a happier place! Just like Reina, you are a special light too! Keep shining, little one!

Reflection:

Can you show me how you shine your light by sharing, helping, or smiling, just like Reina does to make the world a happier place?

Today's Prayer:

Dear God, thank you for making me a little light in the world, just like Reina. Help me to share my smiles and love with others, so we can all shine bright together!

21 JUNE

Spirit-Led Living

Let your heart be happy and love everyone, for God guides you! (1 John 4:7)

Dana loved to play and spread joy to everyone around her. One sunny day, she felt a warm feeling in her heart, like a soft hug. "Let your heart be happy and love everyone," she whispered. Dana smiled and danced with the flowers, sharing love with all her friends. Just like Dana, God wants us to love and be happy!

Reflection:

Can you show me how you let your heart be happy and share love with others, just like Dana does when she dances and smiles with her friends?

Today's Prayer:

Dear God, thank you for filling my heart with happiness and love. Please help me share your joy with everyone around me and let your love shine through me each day.

---

22 JUNE

He Sees Every Tear

God loves you, and He sees every tear you cry. (Psalm 56:8)

Everly felt a little sad when her favorite toy fell. She looked up and whispered, "God, do you see my tears?" In her heart, she felt a warm hug. God did see her tears! He loves her so much and always cares. When you're sad, remember, God sees every tear, and He's right there with you, ready to help you smile again!

Reflection:

When you feel a little sad, like when your toy falls, can you think of a happy thing that makes you smile? What is it?

Today's Prayer:

Dear God, thank You for always seeing my tears and loving me so much. When I feel sad, help me remember that You are right here, ready to make me smile again.

23 JUNE

The Beauty of Dependence

God loves us and takes care of us like a good Shepherd takes care of his sheep. (Psalm 23:1)

Mica loved to play in the green grass, but sometimes she felt a little scared. Then, her good Shepherd came to her! He gently led her to sweet water and soft fields. "You are safe with me, Mica," He said. Just like the Shepherd loves Mica, God loves you too. He takes care of you all the time, saying, "You are never alone. I am here."

Reflection:

Can you show me how you feel safe and cared for, knowing God is your good Shepherd and always with you, just like Mica?

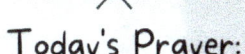

Today's Prayer:

Dear God, thank you for being my good Shepherd and taking care of me all the time. Please help me feel safe and loved, knowing I am never alone with you by my side.

---

24 JUNE

A Life of Overflow

God gives us lots of love to share!
(1 John 4:19)

Thalia had a big heart full of love, just like a balloon filled with air! One day, she discovered that when she shared her love with her friends, her heart felt even bigger! She hugged her teddy, shared her toys, and smiled at everyone. Just like a spring that never runs dry, God fills our hearts with love to share. Let's give away our love and watch it grow!

Reflection:

What do you like to share with your friends to make your heart feel big and happy, just like Thalia?

Today's Prayer:

Dear God, thank you for filling my heart with so much love to share. Please help me give hugs, smiles, and kindness to my friends, so my heart can grow even bigger with your love.

25 JUNE

The Lord Will Provide

The Lord is our helper, and He takes care of us
(Psalm 23:1)

Ruth loved to play and explore, but one day, she felt lonely and lost. Then she heard a gentle voice say, "Don't worry, little one. I am here!" It was her Shepherd, always nearby, taking care of her. Just like the Shepherd loves Ruth, God loves you too! He is our helper and takes care of us always!

Reflection:

Can you show me how you feel safe and cared for, knowing God is always with you and helps you, just like Ruth's Shepherd?

Today's Prayer:

Dear God, thank you for always being with me and taking care of me when I feel lonely or lost. Please help me remember you are my helper and I am never alone.

---

26 JUNE

Standing in Spiritual Authority

You are strong and can do great things with

God's love! (Philippians 4:13)

Nicole had a special magic inside her—God's love! When she felt small, she remembered she could do big things, just like superheroes! One day, she helped a friend who was sad, and her heart felt warm and brave. Nicole whispered, "I am strong!" With God's love, she knew she could do great things every day!

Reflection:

Can you think of a time when you helped someone and felt really brave, just like a superhero? What made your heart feel warm?

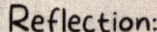

Today's Prayer:

Dear God, thank you for filling me with your love and making me strong inside. Please help me be brave and do great things for others, knowing you are always with me.

27 JUNE

Faith Over Frustration
Trust in God like a bright light in the dark.
(Psalm 56:3)

Crissy felt scared in the dark and wanted to shine bright but couldn't see her way. Then, she remembered her special friend—God! With a big heart, she whispered, "I trust you!" Suddenly, a warm light filled the sky, guiding her home. Just like Crissy, trust in God, and He'll help you shine bright even in the dark!

Reflection:

Can you show me how you trust God to help you shine bright and feel safe, even when things seem a little scary or dark, just like Crissy?

Today's Prayer:

Dear God, thank you for being my light when I feel scared or lost. Please help me trust you and shine bright, knowing you are always guiding me home.

---

28 JUNE

Renewed by Grace
God loves you and makes you new every day!
(2 Corinthians 5:17)

Jessa woke up each morning to feel new, just like a fresh flower in the sun! She danced around with joy, knowing God made her special. Even when she felt sad, she remembered God's love made her clean and bright, like a sunny day. Every day is a new adventure, full of grace and love!

Reflection:

Can you think of a time when you felt happy and special, just like a flower in the sun? What makes you feel that way?

Today's Prayer:

Dear God, thank you for making me new and filling my heart with your love every day. Please help me remember your grace and feel happy and special, just like a flower in the sunshine.

29
JUNE

The Gift of His Presence
God is always with us and loves us very much!
(Psalm 139:7)

Dani was playing all by herself in a big room, feeling a little shy. Then, she remembered something special: God was always with her, like a warm hug. She smiled, feeling His love surround her. "God loves me very much," she whispered, and her heart felt peaceful. Just like Dani, God is always with you!

Reflection:

Can you show me how you feel peaceful and loved, even when you're by yourself, knowing God is always with you just like He is with Dani?

Today's Prayer:

Dear God, thank you for being with me and loving me, even when I am by myself. Please help my heart feel peaceful and safe, knowing you are always close to me.

30
JUNE

Finish Strong in Faith
God loves you all the time!
(1 John 4:16)

Erica loved to hop and play, but sometimes she felt tired. One day, as she sat under a big tree, she remembered, "God loves you all the time!" Erica smiled and stood up again. With each hop, she felt God's love helping her keep going. Just like Erica, you can always finish strong, knowing God loves you!

Reflection:

Can you show me how you keep going and finish strong, even when you feel tired, knowing God loves you just like He loves Erica?

Today's Prayer:

Dear God, thank you for loving me and helping me keep going when I feel tired. Please give me strength to finish strong and remember your love is always with me.

July

Freedom in Christ

Jesus loves you and makes you free!
(John 8:36)

Leanna twirled through the garden, her arms out like wings. She laughed and sang, "Jesus loves me and sets me free!" The sunshine tickled her cheeks, and the breeze whispered through the flowers. With every spin, her heart felt lighter and happier. She waved to the butterflies and danced with joy. Even the little bunny nearby seemed to hop along with her happiness.

Just like Leanna, you can feel free and full of love too! Jesus fills your heart with joy, and His love helps you shine bright. Whether you're twirling, resting, or just smiling, His love is always with you, making your heart feel happy and light.

Reflection:

Can you show me how you feel happy and free, knowing Jesus loves you and helps your heart shine bright, just like Leanna does when she twirls in the garden?

Today's Prayer:

Dear Jesus, thank you for loving me and making my heart feel happy and free. Please help me shine bright with your joy and remember your love is always with me.

2 JULY

God's Love Never Fails

God loves you always, and His love never ends!
(Psalm 136:1)

Dulce loves to play and laugh with her friends. Sometimes, things go wrong or she feels sad, but God's love never stops. God loves Dulce all the time, no matter what happens! Every day, Dulce can remember that God's love is always there, like a warm hug. She is never alone because God's love never fails or goes away.

Reflection:

Can you show me how you feel safe and happy, Knowing God loves you all the time, just like Dulce does even when things go wrong?

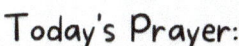

Today's Prayer:

Dear God, thank you for loving me all the time, no matter what happens. Please help me feel safe and happy, Knowing your love never goes away.

---

3 JULY

Courage to Follow God's Call

Be strong and brave; God is with you wherever you go!
(Joshua 1:9)

Aliza heard God's whisper, "Be strong and brave; I am with you!" Her heart felt big and happy! She climbed the tall slide, twirled like a butterfly, and shared her toy with a friend. Even when she felt shy, she smiled, remembering God was with her. She followed His call with joy!

Reflection:

When you feel a little shy like Aliza, what fun thing can you do to be brave and share your smile with a friend?

Today's Prayer:

Dear God, thank you for always being with me, just like you promised. Help me be strong and brave, so I can share, play, and follow your happy whispers in my heart.

4
JULY

True Freedom Through Faith

You are free to be happy because God loves you! (John 8:36)

Janelle loved to twirl in the sunshine and giggle with her friends. One day, she felt a happy whisper in her heart: "You are free to be happy because God loves you!" Janelle clapped her hands and danced with joy. Just like Janelle, you are special—and God's love makes your heart light and free!

Reflection:

When you spin around like Janelle in the sunshine, how does it make your heart feel? Can you feel God's love making you happy while you twirl?

Today's Prayer:

Dear God, thank you for your love that makes our hearts feel light and free. Help us to twirl and giggle with joy, knowing that we are happy because you are always with us.

5
JULY

Faith in the Everyday

God loves you, and He is always with you! (Psalm 139:7)

Andrea loved to play outside and collect shiny rocks. One day, she found a sparkly one and said, "What a special treasure!" Just like that rock, Andrea is special to God! He loves her so much and is always with her. Whether she's playing or resting, God is right there, loving her every day!

Reflection:

Can you show me how you feel special and loved by God, just like Andrea does when she finds a shiny treasure?

Today's Prayer:

Dear God, thank you for loving me and making me your special treasure. Please help me remember you are always with me, whether I am playing or resting.

6 JULY

Abiding in Peace

God gives us peace in our hearts.
(Philippians 4:7)

Little grasshopper named Ava loved to jump and explore, but sometimes she felt nervous. One day, her friend the wise ladybug told her, "When you're scared, close your eyes and think of happy things. God gives us peace in our hearts." Ava thought of soft leaves and sunny skies, and she felt cozy inside! Just like Ava, we can feel God's peace whenever we need it.

Reflection:

When you feel a little nervous, what happy things can you think of to help you feel cozy and peaceful like Ava?

Today's Prayer:

Dear God, thank you for giving me peace in my heart when I feel nervous or scared. Please help me remember happy things and feel your love, so I can feel cozy and safe inside.

---

7 JULY

Living for an Audience of One

Do everything to make God happy!
(Colossians 3:23)

Inka the cricket loved to sing, hopping from leaf to leaf. She wanted her song to be the sweetest, not just for her friends, but to make God smile. As she chirped in the sunshine, she thought, "I'm doing this for God!" Inka learned that when we do things for God, we feel happy inside. Let's all do our best to make God smile!

Reflection:

What is your favorite song to sing or dance to? Can you think of a way to make God smile when you share it, just like Inka the cricket?

Today's Prayer:

Dear God, thank you for giving me songs to sing and ways to make you smile. Please help me do my best in everything, so my heart can be happy and bring you joy.

8 JULY

Finding Stillness with God

God is with you, and He loves you very much.
(Psalm 46:10)

Betsy the beetle loved to scurry around, but sometimes she felt busy inside. One day, she found a soft spot under a big leaf and sat very still. As she listened to the wind, she remembered, "God is with me, and He loves me very much." Just like the quiet breeze, God's love made Betsy feel peaceful. When you're still, you can feel God's love too!

Reflection:

Can you find a cozy spot like Betsy the beetle? What do you feel inside when you sit very still and think about God loving you?

Today's Prayer:

Dear God, thank you for being with me and loving me so much. Please help me find quiet moments to sit still and feel your peaceful love in my heart.

---

9 JULY

The Strength of Surrender

God helps me when I let go and trust Him!
(Psalm 55:22)

Izzy the iguana wanted to climb high, but she felt scared. Then she remembered that when she trusted the sturdy branches below, they would hold her steady. Just like Izzy, when we let go of our worries and trust God, He helps us feel strong and safe. So, let's trust God to help us climb higher!

Reflection:

What do you think it feels like to let go of being scared, just like Izzy did? Can you share a time when you felt brave like her?

Today's Prayer:

Dear God, thank you for helping me feel strong and safe when I let go of my worries. Please help me trust you and be brave, just like Izzy the iguana.

10 JULY

Becoming a Woman of Influence

Be kind and help others, just like Jesus!
(Ephesians 4:32)

Lyra loved to play and share with her friends. One day, she saw a sad bunny and remembered to be kind, just like Jesus said. So, she picked some flowers and gave them to the bunny, making him smile! Just like Lyra, you can be kind and help others, spreading joy everywhere you go!

Reflection:

Can you show me how you spread joy and kindness to others, just like Lyra did when she helped the sad bunny?

Today's Prayer:

Dear Jesus, thank you for teaching me to be kind and help others. Please help me spread joy and share your love with everyone I meet.

---

11 JULY

Trust When You Can't See

God is with you, even when you can't see Him!
(Psalm 139:7)

Amor loved playing hide and seek, but sometimes she felt scared when she couldn't see her friends. Then, she remembered that God was always with her, even when she couldn't see Him! Like a cozy blanket, God's love wrapped around her. So when you feel lost, trust, because God is holding you close!

Reflection:

Can you show me how you feel safe and loved, even when you can't see your friends, knowing God is always with you just like He is with Amor?

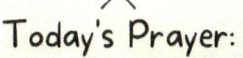

Today's Prayer:

Dear God, thank you for being with me and holding me close, even when I can't see you or my friends. Please help me feel safe and loved, trusting that you are always near.

12 JULY

Grace That Covers All
God's love is big and covers everything!
(1 Peter 4:8)

Leia loves to snuggle under her soft, cozy blanket. It wraps all around her and makes her feel safe and warm. God's love is even bigger than Leia's blanket! No matter what happens, God's love covers everything and keeps Leia safe. Every day, Leia can remember that God's grace is always with her, wrapping her in love.

Reflection:

Can you show me how you feel safe and warm, knowing God's love wraps all around you like a big, cozy blanket, just like Leia?

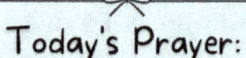

Today's Prayer:

Dear God, thank you for wrapping me in your big love and keeping me safe and warm. Please help me remember your grace is always with me, no matter what happens.

---

13 JULY

Letting God Lead
God loves you and will show you the way!
(Psalm 32:8)

Tasha loved to play outside, but sometimes she felt unsure of where to go. One day, she heard a gentle voice saying, "Don't worry, Tasha! I love you and will show you the way!" Tasha looked up and saw a bright path shining ahead. She followed the light, knowing God was leading her. Just like Tasha, God will show you the way too!

Reflection:

Can you show me how you follow God's light and trust Him to show you the way, just like Tasha did when she saw the bright path?

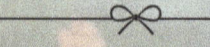

Today's Prayer:

Dear God, thank you for loving me and showing me the way when I feel unsure. Please help me follow your light and trust you to lead me every step I take.

14 JULY

Rejoicing in Trials

Be happy, little one, even when things are tough! (James 1:2)

Marley was walking through the garden when she stepped in a muddy puddle! Oh no, her shoes got dirty! But instead of feeling upset, she giggled and splashed in the mud. Marley remembered that even when things get tricky, she could still be happy. Just like Marley, you can smile and find joy, no matter what!

Reflection:

When you see a muddy puddle, what fun things can you do to make you smile, just like Marley did?

Today's Prayer:

Dear God, thank you for helping me find happiness, even when things are messy or hard. Please fill my heart with joy so I can smile and have fun, no matter what comes my way.

---

15 JULY

The Power of Spiritual Discipline

Doing good things makes your heart happy! (Galatians 6:9)

Freya loved to share her toys with her friends. Every time she shared, her heart felt warm and happy, like a cozy blanket. One day, Freya helped a friend pick up their blocks, and her smile shone bright. Just like Freya, you can make your heart happy by doing good things and showing love every day!

Reflection:

What is something kind you can do for a friend today that will make your heart feel warm and happy, just like Freya?

Today's Prayer:

Dear God, thank you for helping me do good things and show love to my friends. Please help my heart feel warm and happy every time I share and help others.

16 JULY

Your Past Does Not Define You
You are special and loved, always!
(1 John 3:1)

Francine sometimes felt sad about things that happened before. But one day, she met Wise Owl, who said, "Francine, you are special and loved, always!" Francine realized that her past didn't matter. What mattered was her heart, shining bright with love. Just like Francine, you are special and loved no matter what!

Reflection:

Can you think of a time when you felt a little sad, just like Francine? What makes your heart feel happy and special now?

───────✗───────

Today's Prayer:

Dear God, thank you for loving me and making me special, no matter what happened before. Please help my heart shine bright with your love and fill me with happiness each day.

---

17 JULY

Choosing Joy Over Anxiety
Choose to be happy, for God loves you!
(Philippians 4:4)

Amelia loved to play and laugh, but sometimes little worries tried to make her feel sad. One day, she remembered what God said: "Choose to be happy, for I love you!" So, Amelia wiggled her toes, took a deep breath, and danced in the sunshine. She decided to choose joy, even when worries came! You can too!

Reflection:

Can you show me how you choose to be happy and dance, even when you feel a little worried, just like Amelia does in the sunshine?

───────✗───────

Today's Prayer:

Dear God, thank you for loving me and helping me choose joy when I feel worried. Please fill my heart with happiness and help me dance through every day with your love.

18
JULY

Delight in the Lord
Be happy in the Lord!
(Psalms 37:4)

Mina twirled and danced in the sunshine, feeling so happy. She knew that God loved her very much, just like the flowers in the garden. When Mina smiled and shared her joy, it made God happy too! She laughed and played, knowing that the Lord delights in her laughter. Let's all be happy in the Lord, just like Mina!

Reflection:

Can you show me how you smile and share your joy, knowing God is happy when you are happy, just like Mina in the sunshine?

Today's Prayer:

Dear God, thank you for loving me and being happy when I smile and share my joy. Please help me delight in you and fill my days with laughter and sunshine.

19
JULY

Finding Balance in God's Design
God made everything just right, and He loves you so much! (Genesis 1:31)

Kendra loved to laugh, play, and rest, just like the world God made. She knew that God created everything perfectly, including her! Whether she was running in the sunshine or resting in the shade, Kendra felt balanced and loved. Just like Kendra, you are part of God's beautiful design!

Reflection:

Can you show me how you feel happy and loved, whether you're playing or resting, knowing God made you just right, just like Kendra?

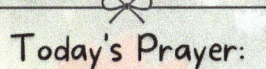

Today's Prayer:

Dear God, thank you for making me just right and loving me so much. Please help me feel your love and joy, whether I am playing or resting, and remember I am part of your beautiful design.

20 JULY

Hope in the Wilderness

God is with us even in the wild places.
(Isaiah 43:2)

Phoebe was exploring the big forest when it felt a little scary. But then she remembered, "God is with me!" As she walked, she saw colorful flowers and playful creatures. The sun peeked through the trees, and Phoebe felt safe and happy. Just like Phoebe, you can trust that God is always with you, even in wild places.

Reflection:

Can you show me how you feel safe and happy, even in new or wild places, knowing God is always with you just like He is with Phoebe?

— ✗ —

Today's Prayer:

Dear God, thank you for being with me wherever I go, even in new or wild places. Please help me feel safe and happy, trusting that you are always by my side.

---

21 JULY

You Are God's Masterpiece

You are wonderfully made by God and so very special!
(Psalm 139:14)

God painted a beautiful picture, and that picture was Wendy! He used sparkly colors for her laughter and soft pastels for her hugs. Every day, Wendy is a wonderful masterpiece, made with love. Just like a bright flower, she shines with God's love, special and loved in every way.

Reflection:

Dear God, thank you for making me your special masterpiece, full of bright and happy colors. Please help me shine with your love and remember how wonderful and loved I am every day.

— ✗ —

Today's Prayer:

Dear God, thank you for making me your special masterpiece, full of bright and happy colors. Please help me shine with your love and remember how wonderful and loved I am every day.

22 JULY

Living Loved and Known
You are so special and loved by God!
(1 John 3:1)

In a bright, colorful garden, there lived a little girl named Sadie. Sometimes, Sadie wondered if she was special. One sunny day, her mom gently whispered, "You are so special and loved by God!" Sadie felt warm and happy, knowing she was perfect just as she was. Just like Sadie, you are loved and known by God!

Reflection:

When you think about how much God loves you, what makes you feel special like Sadie in her colorful garden?

Today's Prayer:

Dear God, thank you for making me special and loved just like Sadie in the garden. Help me feel your love every day, knowing I am perfect just as I am.

---

23 JULY

The Voice That Calms
Jesus loves you and calms your heart!
(Mark 4:39)

The waves were big and splashed everywhere, and Lydia felt scared. But Jesus said, "Be still!" And just like that, the waves stopped. Jesus loves you, Lydia! When you feel scared or worried, remember Jesus is with you. Close your eyes and think of Him saying, "I love you. I'm here." His love makes you feel calm and happy, just like the quiet sea.

Reflection:

When you see big waves or hear loud noises, can you close your eyes and think of Jesus saying, "I love you"? How does that make your heart feel?

Today's Prayer:

Dear Jesus, thank you for loving me and calming my heart when I feel scared or worried. Please help me remember you are always with me, bringing peace and happiness inside.

24
JULY

Returning to Your First Love

God loves you so much, always come back to Him with a happy heart! ❤️ (Revelation 2:4)

Annalise loves to run and play, but sometimes she gets busy and forgets to talk to God. God always loves Annalise and wants her to come back to Him with a happy heart. When Annalise remembers God and says, "I love you," her heart feels warm and close to Him. Every day, Annalise can return to God's love and feel joyful.

Reflection:

Can you show me how you come back to God with a happy heart and say, "I love you," just like Annalise does when she remembers Him?

Today's Prayer:

Dear God, thank you for always loving me and waiting for me with open arms. Please help me come back to you with a happy heart and say, "I love you," every day.

25
JULY

Perseverance Through Prayer

Always keep asking God, and He will help you! (Luke 11:9)

Rebecca loved to play and build towers with blocks, but sometimes she needed help. She remembered her friend saying, "Always ask God, and He will help you!" So, Rebecca clasped her hands, whispered her wish, and each time she prayed, her tower grew taller! Just like Rebecca, keep praying, and God will help you!

Reflection:

When you are building your block tower and it feels wobbly, what do you like to say to God to help you make it tall?

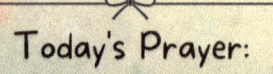

Today's Prayer:

Dear God, thank you for helping me build my towers each day. When I ask you for help, I know you listen and make my dreams come true!

26
JULY

Flourishing in Every Season

Like a little flower, you can grow and be happy in every season! (Psalm 1:3)

Carm loved playing in her sunny garden. Some days it rained, and other days the sun shined bright. But Carm smiled in every kind of weather! She danced in puddles and twirled in the sunshine. Just like a flower, Carm was blooming with joy. God helps you grow and smile in every season, too!

Reflection:

What's your favorite way to play when it's sunny and when it rains? Can you think of a fun dance for each kind of weather?

Today's Prayer:

Dear God, thank you for helping me grow and be happy in every season, whether it's sunny or rainy. Please help me find joy and keep blooming with your love no matter what the weather is like.

27
JULY

God's Presence in Your Routine

God is with you everywhere you go!
(Psalm 139:7)

Clarissa danced from room to room, giggling as she played with her toys. In the garden, she picked flowers and felt God's love like a cozy blanket. When she splashed in puddles, she knew God was splashing too! Wherever you go, just like Clarissa, remember—God is always with you!

Reflection:

When you dance and giggle like Clarissa, where do you feel God's love around you? Is it when you're playing, picking flowers, or splashing in puddles?

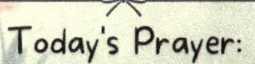

Today's Prayer:

Dear God, thank you for being with me everywhere I go and filling my days with your love. Please help me feel your cozy hugs whether I'm playing, picking flowers, or splashing in puddles.

28
JULY

Living with Holy Confidence
You are special and loved; God is always with you! (Psalm 139:14)

Emerald felt special and loved. She knew God was with her, like a cozy blanket on a chilly day. When she felt shy or scared, she smiled and said, "I am made wonderfully!" With every hop and twirl, she danced with joy. Just like Emerald, you are special—God is always by your side!

Reflection:

When you hop and twirl like Emerald, how does it feel to know that God is always by your side making you feel special and loved?

Today's Prayer:

Dear God, thank you for making me special and always being by my side. Please help me feel your love and dance with joy, knowing you are with me wherever I go.

29
JULY

Releasing the Weights You Carry
Let go and be happy, for Jesus loves you so much! (1 Peter 5:7)

Eden carried a big, heavy bag filled with frowns and worries. One sunny day, she remembered, "Jesus loves me!" So, she let go of her bag and felt light as a feather! Eden danced and giggled, so happy and free. Just like Eden, you can let go too— Jesus loves you and makes your heart joyful!

Reflection:

Can you show me how you let go of your worries and feel light and happy, knowing Jesus loves you just like He loves Eden?

Today's Prayer:

Dear Jesus, thank you for loving me and helping me let go of my worries. Please fill my heart with joy and help me feel light and free, just like Eden.

30 JULY

Faith That Transforms

With faith, we can do amazing things!
(Matthew 17:20)

Tiny seeds rested in the ground, waiting to grow. With sunshine and rain, they became tall flowers, dancing in the breeze! Just like the flowers, Issa's faith helped her grow, too. When she believed, she shared, cared, and loved big! With a little faith, amazing things can happen—even today!

Reflection:

Can you show me how you use your faith to do something amazing, like sharing or caring for someone, just like Issa and the flowers that grow tall?

Today's Prayer:

Dear God, thank you for giving me faith that helps me grow and do wonderful things. Please help me share, care, and love others, trusting that even my little faith can make amazing things happen.

---

31 JULY

Praise Before the Breakthrough

Sing and be happy because God loves you!
(Psalm 147:1)

In a bright, cheerful forest, all the animals sang with joy because they knew God loved them. Yassi twirled and clapped, singing, "God loves me!" Even the shy turtle joined in. When a storm came, they kept singing. And then—sunshine and a rainbow! Keep singing, little one—God's love is always there!

Reflection:

When you feel happy like Yassi and all the animals in the forest, what songs do you like to sing to show how much you love God?

Today's Prayer:

Dear God, thank you for filling my heart with songs and joy, even when things are hard. Please help me keep singing and praising you, knowing your love is always with me.

August

AUGUST 1

Rooted in God's Truth
God loves you very much!
(1 John 4:9)

A little girl named Nessa loved to twirl through the garden, just like the happy flowers. She smiled at the sunshine and giggled when butterflies danced nearby. Nessa knew deep in her heart that God loved her very much! Just like the sun helps flowers grow, God's love made Nessa's heart feel bright and full of joy.

As she played, Nessa waved to the birds and patted the soft grass. She felt strong and safe, like her feet were planted in God's love. Even on cloudy days, she remembered that love never changes. Nessa was special, precious, and always rooted in God's big, warm love.

Reflection:

Can you show me how you feel strong and joyful, knowing God's love helps you grow and keeps you safe, just like Nessa in the garden?

———— ✄ ————

Today's Prayer:
Dear God, thank you for loving me and helping me grow strong and joyful. Please keep my heart rooted in your love so I always feel safe and happy, just like Nessa.

———— ✄ ————

2
AUGUST

Confidence in His Plan

God has a good plan for you!
(Jeremiah 29:11)

A little girl named Maliyah loved to sing and play. One day, she felt a little scared to try something new. But she remembered, "God has a good plan for me!" So, she smiled, took a deep breath, and gave it a try. Just like that, Maliyah felt brave! God's plan is always full of love and joy!

Reflection:

Maliyah had a brave moment, didn't she? When you try something new, what makes you feel happy and brave like Maliyah?

Today's Prayer:

Dear God, thank you for having a good plan for me and helping me feel brave. Please fill my heart with happiness and courage whenever I try something new.

3
AUGUST

When You Feel Spiritually Dry

God loves you always, just like the rain makes flowers grow! (Psalm 104:13)

Rylee stood in her garden feeling quiet and a little dry inside. She looked at the sky and whispered, "God, I need You." Then, soft clouds rolled in, and gentle rain began to fall. Rylee twirled and laughed! Just like the rain helps flowers grow, God's love helps our hearts feel strong and happy again!

Reflection:

Can you show me how you ask God for help and let His love make your heart happy, just like rain helps flowers grow?our happy come back? Do you like to dance, play, or look at the sky like Rylee?

Today's Prayer:

Dear God, thank you for loving me and making my heart happy again. Please help me grow strong in your love, like flowers in the rain.

4
AUGUST

God Is in the Details
God loves every little thing He made!
(Psalm 139:14)

In a bright, colorful world, Jolie looked at the fluffy clouds, the tiny ants, and the little flowers blooming in spring. She smiled, knowing that God made all these things—and made her, too! From her tiny toes to her sparkling eyes, God loves every little thing about her. Just like the butterfly, God is in all the details, loving you so much!

Reflection:

Can you point to something small and say, "God made this and loves me too!" just like Jolie does with the flowers and clouds?

———————— ✄ ————————

Today's Prayer:

Dear God, thank you for making every little thing and loving me so much. Help me see your love in all the details around me.

———————— • ————————

5
AUGUST

Letting Go of the Past
Jesus loves you and helps you keep looking forward! (Philippians 3:13)

Little Elena found a big, shiny balloon that made her so happy! But one day, the balloon floated away. Elena felt sad, until she heard a gentle voice, "Jesus loves you, Elena!" it said. "Let go of the balloon and look ahead!" Elena smiled, feeling light and joyful, knowing Jesus helps her look forward with a happy heart!

Reflection:

Can you show me how you let go of something sad and look ahead with a happy heart, just like Elena did?

———————— ✄ ————————

Today's Prayer:

Dear Jesus, thank you for loving me and helping me let go of sad things. Please fill my heart with joy as I look ahead with you.

6
AUGUST

Choosing Faith in Uncertainty
God is with you always, even when you feel scared. (Isaiah 41:10)

Abby, a little butterfly, fluttered in the big, wide world. Sometimes, she felt scared in the tall grass and dark trees. But then, she remembered: "God is with me always!" She spread her wings, singing, "God is by my side!" Just like Abby, you can choose faith, trusting that God is with you, making everything bright and safe.

Reflection:

Can you show me how you feel brave and safe, trusting God is with you, just like Abby the butterfly?

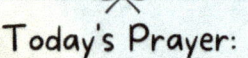

Today's Prayer:

Dear God, thank you for being with me when I feel scared. Help me trust you and feel brave, knowing you are always by my side.

7
AUGUST

You Are Seen and Known
God sees you and loves you very much! (Psalm 139:1)

Little Nova danced in the breeze of a bright, colorful garden, wondering if anyone noticed her. A friendly firefly fluttered by and whispered, "Oh, Nova, God sees you! He knows everything about you and loves you so much." Nova smiled, feeling warm inside. Just like her, God sees and loves you too! You are special!

Reflection:

Can you show me your happy smile, knowing God sees you and loves you so much, just like Nova in the garden?

Today's Prayer:

Dear God, thank you for seeing me and loving me so much. Please help me remember I am special to you every single day.

8
AUGUST

The Strength of Quiet Obedience

Listen and be calm; God loves you so much!
(Psalm 46:10)

Little Rosa loved to hop and play, but sometimes she got really noisy. One day, she found a cozy spot under a big tree. She sat still and felt the soft breeze. Then she remembered, "God loves me!" Rosa whispered, "I will be calm and listen." In the quiet, her heart felt strong and happy—just like yours can too!

Reflection:

Can you think of a time when you were really quiet and felt happy? What do you like to do when you sit still and listen?

Today's Prayer:

Dear God, thank you for loving me and helping me feel strong and happy when I am quiet and listen to you.

9
AUGUST

Refined by Fire

You are precious and special, like gold shining bright! (1 Peter 1:7)

In a land of sparkly treasures, little Reese felt like a scared gold coin. Then a kind fairy whispered, "You are precious, like gold shining bright!" She sprinkled sparkles, and Reese saw that heat and shaping helped her shine. Just like that, challenges help you glow brighter, sweet treasure!

Reflection:

What makes you feel like a shiny treasure when things feel a little tough?

Today's Prayer:

Dear God, thank you for making me precious and helping me shine, even when things are tough. Please help me glow bright with your love.

10
AUGUST

God's Grace in Your Weakness
God loves you so much, and He helps you when you need it! (2 Corinthians 12:9)

Tasha felt small and droopy like a tiny flower. "I can't stand tall," she sighed. But the breeze whispered, "God loves you and helps you grow." She smiled, feeling strong and safe inside. Just like Tasha, you can shine bright with God's love wrapped all around you!

Reflection:

Can you show me how you feel strong and safe, knowing God's love helps you grow, just like Tasha the tiny flower?

Today's Prayer:

Dear God, thank you for loving me and helping me grow strong. Please wrap me in your love and help me shine bright every day.

11
AUGUST

Living Intentionally
*Always do your best and be kind to others!
(Colossians 3:23)*

Scarlett wanted to be the best girl she could be. She helped her friends, shared her snacks, and gave the sweetest hugs. She remembered, "Always do your best and be kind!" So each day, Scarlett's love made the world shine brighter. Just like her, you can spread kindness, too!

Reflection:

What is one kind thing you can do today to make your friends smile, just like Scarlett?

Today's Prayer:

Dear God, help me do my best and be kind today. Please show me ways to make my friends smile and share your love.

12 AUGUST

The Joy of the Lord Is Your Strength

God makes you happy, and His happiness helps you be strong! (Nehemiah 8:10)

Mabel loved to giggle and play! One sunny day, she picked flowers and danced with butterflies. She felt so happy! Then she remembered a special secret: "God makes you happy, and His happiness helps you be strong!" Mabel smiled even wider, knowing God's joy made her heart strong and unstoppable!

Reflection:

Can you show me your biggest smile and tell me what makes you feel strong and happy, just like Mabel dancing in the sun?

Today's Prayer:

Dear God, thank you for filling my heart with joy and strength. Help me smile big and feel happy, knowing your love makes me strong!

---

13 AUGUST

Clinging to What Is Good

Hold on tight to what is good!
(Romans 12:9)

Cara loved to hop and play, always clinging to her favorite things: her soft blanket, shiny red ball, and cuddly teddy bear. One sunny day, she found shiny butterflies and colorful flowers. She squealed with joy, holding tight to what made her happy! Just like Cara, we can hold on tight to all the good things God gives us.

Reflection:

Can you tell me about your favorite toy or blanket? How does it make you feel when you play with it?

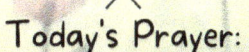

Today's Prayer:

Dear God, thank you for all the good things you give me. Help me hold on tight to your love and share my joy with others!

14 AUGUST

Faithful in the Small Things

Doing little things with love makes God happy!
(Luke 16:10)

In a cozy little garden, there lived a tiny flower named Angelique. She was small but loved sharing her pretty colors with everyone. Every day, she opened her petals and whispered kind words to the busy bees and butterflies. As Angelique sang her sweet song, she made God smile. Little things done with love make God happy!

Reflection:

Can you show me a little thing you can do with love, like sharing a smile or kind words, just like Angelique the tiny flower?

Today's Prayer:

Dear God, help me do little things with love, like sharing smiles and kind words, so I can make you happy every day.

---

15 AUGUST

Renewing Your Mind

God makes our hearts happy and helps us think good thoughts! (Romans 12:2)

A bright, happy forest was home to a little girl named Cindy, who learned a special secret. When Cindy felt sad, she thought of flowers, rainbows, and cuddly friends. She remembered that God makes our hearts happy and helps us think good thoughts! Cindy smiled, danced, and felt joyful inside.

Reflection:

What makes your heart happy like Cindy? Can you think of one special thing that helps you feel brave to let go of sad feelings?

Today's Prayer:

Dear God, thank you for helping me think good thoughts and feel happy inside. Please fill my mind with your joy and love always.

16 AUGUST

The Beauty of Surrender

God loves when we trust Him, like a little bird flying free! (Psalm 37:5)

There was a little girl named Ariana who loved to twirl and dance like a bird in the sky. One day, she lifted her arms and imagined flying free, just like her birdie friends. She thought, "God loves me, and I can trust Him!" When we let go and trust God, He helps our hearts feel light and happy—just like flying!

Reflection:

Can you show me how you let go and trust God, feeling light and happy like a bird flying in the sky, just like Ariana?

Today's Prayer:

Dear God, thank you for helping my heart feel light and free when I trust you. Help me let go and soar with your love today.

---

17 AUGUST

He Works All Things for Good

God makes everything happy for us!
(Romans 8:28)

A bright and colorful garden had a little girl named Norah who knew God was always helping her. When it rained, she felt a little sad—but soon the sun peeked out, and the flowers danced! Norah smiled, knowing God made it all okay. Just like Norah, we can trust that God makes everything happy for us!

Reflection:

When you see a rainbow or flowers after the rain, what makes you feel happy like Norah?

Today's Prayer:

Dear God, thank you for the beautiful flowers and the happy sun that shines bright. Help us remember that even when it rains, you are with us, making everything joyful and good!

18
AUGUST

A Steadfast Spirit
God gives us strong hearts and happy spirits!
(Psalm 51:10)

Madeline loved to laugh and play with her friends. One day, she felt a little shy and held her mommy's hand. "It's okay," Mommy said. "God gives us strong hearts and happy spirits!" Madeline took a deep breath, felt brave, and joined the fun. Just like Madeline, you can be strong and joyful with God's help!

Reflection:

Can you show me how you feel brave and joyful, knowing God gives you a strong heart, just like Madeline?

Today's Prayer:

Dear God, thank you for giving me a strong heart and a happy spirit. Help me be brave and joyful, even when I feel shy.

19
AUGUST

Hope That Holds
God's love is like a warm hug, bringing us hope every day! (Romans 15:13)

A fluffy cloud named Hope loved to float through the sky, sharing warm hugs with everyone below. "God loves you so much!" she sang. Flowers smiled, birds chirped, and trees danced. When Paula felt sad, she looked up and saw Hope's hugs, reminding her that love always makes everything better.

Reflection:

When you see a fluffy cloud in the sky, what do you think it might be saying to you?

Today's Prayer:

Dear God, thank you for your love that feels like a warm hug. When I feel sad, help me remember your hope and smile again.

20 AUGUST

Casting Your Cares

God loves you and helps you when you're feeling sad! (1 Peter 5:7)

Gabby had a soft teddy bear she hugged when she felt sad. One day, she whispered, "God, I feel blue." A gentle breeze wrapped her in warmth. "God loves you and helps you!" it seemed to say. Gabby shared her sad feelings like sharing cookies—and her heart felt light and happy again!

Reflection:

When you feel a little sad, who do you like to hug, just like Gabby hugged her teddy bear? How does that make you feel?

Today's Prayer:

Dear God, thank you for loving me and helping me when I feel sad. Please hold my heart and make it light and happy again.

---

21 AUGUST

He Is with You Always

God is with you all the time! (Matthew 28:20)

Myla loved to play and explore outside. One day at the big park, she felt a little scared. Then she remembered, "God is with you all the time!" She talked to God in her heart and felt brave and happy. Just like Myla, you can remember God is always with you —watching over you with love!

Reflection:

Can you show me how you feel brave and happy, knowing God is with you all the time, just like Myla at the park?

Today's Prayer:

Dear God, thank you for being with me all the time. Help me feel brave and happy, knowing your love is always watching over me.

22
AUGUST

Walking in the Light
Walk in the light and be happy!
(1 John 1:7)

Kali loved to play in the bright sunshine. "Walking in the light makes me feel so happy!" she said. One day, she found a dark cave and felt a little scared. But then she walked back into the warm sun. Kali danced and twirled with joy! Just like Kali, we can choose to walk in the light and feel happy inside!

Reflection:

When you feel the warm sunshine on your face, how does it make you want to dance and play?

Today's Prayer:

Dear God, thank you for the warm sunshine that makes us happy and helps us feel safe. Help us remember to walk in the light, just like Kali, so we can dance and twirl with joy every day.

23
AUGUST

Forgiveness Is Freedom
Forgive others, just like God forgives you!
(Matthew 6:12)

Vania had a friend named Benny who stepped on her favorite toy. She felt sad and wanted to be mad. But then she remembered how God forgives us! So, Vania chose to forgive Benny. Her heart felt light and happy, like a balloon! Forgiving sets us free—just like God sets us free with His big love!

Reflection:

Can you show me how you forgive someone and feel your heart light and happy, just like Vania did with Benny?

Today's Prayer:

Dear God, thank you for forgiving me and helping me forgive others. Please fill my heart with your love and set me free with your joy.

24
AUGUST

Bearing Spiritual Fruit

We can be kind and loving, like flowers that grow!
(John 15:5)

Little flowers swayed in the breeze, sharing smiles with everyone. Kaia watched them and giggled. "I want to be kind like the flowers!" she said. So, she helped her friend and gave sweet hugs. Just like the flowers bloom in the sun, Kaia's heart bloomed with love. You can grow kindness too!

Reflection:

What nice things can you do today to help your friends feel happy, just like the flowers make you smile?

Today's Prayer:

Dear God, help me grow kindness and love in my heart. Show me ways to make my friends happy, just like blooming flowers.

25
AUGUST

The Peace of Letting Go

Let it go and be happy, for God takes care of you!(1 Peter 5:7)

In a sunny garden, Mara found a shiny leaf she loved so much! She held it tight, but the wind made her feel worried. A wise frog said, "Let it go, little one! God takes care of you!" So, Mara let it fly, and her heart felt light and happy. Letting go brings peace, and God always cares for you!

Reflection:

Can you show me how you let go of something and feel happy and light, knowing God takes care of you, just like Mara?

Today's Prayer:

Dear God, thank you for taking care of me. Help me let go of my worries and feel happy and light, trusting in your love.

26
AUGUST

Strength to Begin Again
God helps us try again and be strong!
(Philippians 4:13)

Haley loved to jump and twirl, but sometimes she fell down. Instead of feeling sad, she remembered—God helps us try again! With a brave heart, Haley stood up, smiled, and gave it another go. "I can do it!" she cheered. And she did! Just like Haley, you can always begin again with God's help!

Reflection:

When you jump and twirl like Haley, what do you feel in your heart when you try again after a fall?

Today's Prayer:

Dear God, thank you for helping me try again and be strong. Please give me courage to stand up and smile after I fall.

27
AUGUST

Your Life Is a Testimony
Let your light shine so others can see how good God is! (Matthew 5:16)

Mina loved to smile and share her happiness with everyone. One day, she learned that her kindness made others feel happy too! When Mina was loving and kind, it made the world shine brighter, just like a little light in the dark. Just like Mina, you can shine your light and show everyone how good God is!

Reflection:

Can you show me how you shine your light by being kind and loving, just like Mina, so others can see how good God is?

Today's Prayer:

Dear God, help me shine your light by being kind and loving. Let others see your goodness through my words and actions.

28
AUGUST

Restoring Joy
God will fill our hearts with happiness!
(Psalm 51:12)

Bridget felt a little sad one day when the flowers in the garden didn't bloom. She whispered, "Please help me feel happy again!" And guess what? God filled her heart with sunshine! Suddenly, the flowers danced, and Bridget giggled with joy! Just like Bridget, when you feel sad, remember, God will fill your heart with happiness!

Reflection:

Can you show me how you ask God to help you feel happy again, just like Bridget did when the flowers didn't bloom?

———————✄———————

Today's Prayer:

Dear God, thank you for filling my heart with happiness when I feel sad. Please help me find your sunshine and joy each day.

———————●———————

29
AUGUST

God's Power in Your Story
God loves you very much and is always with you! (Psalm 139:5)

Kallie loved to play and dream big! One day, she saw a beautiful rainbow and remembered that God loves her very much. Just like the rainbow, God is always with her, holding her hand through every adventure. When Kallie felt scared, she whispered, "God's power is in my story!" And she felt brave! Just like Kallie, God is with you in every fun moment!

Reflection:

Can you show me how you feel brave and happy, knowing God is with you in every adventure, just like Kallie and her rainbow?

———————✄———————

Today's Prayer:

Dear God, thank you for being with me in every adventure. Help me feel brave and happy, knowing your love is always holding my hand.

30 AUGUST

Enduring with Grace
You can do hard things with God's help!
(Philippians 4:13)

LyKa wanted to grow tall, but the wind blew hard, and the rain fell heavy. LyKa felt scared, but then she remembered: "You can do hard things with God's help!" So, she took a deep breath and stood strong. With God's loving care, she pushed through and reached for the sun. Just like LyKa, you can do hard things with God's help!

Reflection:

Can you show me how you stand strong and brave, Knowing God helps you do hard things, just like LyKa reaching for the sun?

⤜✿⤛

Today's Prayer:

Dear God, thank you for helping me be strong and brave. Please stay with me and help me do hard things with your love.

⬤

31 AUGUST

Preparing for a New Season
God makes everything beautiful in its time.
(Ecclesiastes 3:11)

In a garden full of colors, flowers were waking up. The sun said, "It's time to bloom!" Little Serena stood tall and smiled, Knowing she was made beautiful by God. Each moment felt just right, like a new season. Soon, her friends would join, and the garden would shine. Remember, Serena, God makes everything lovely in its time!

Reflection:

Can you show me how you get ready for something new, trusting God will make it beautiful, just like Serena in the garden?

⤜✿⤛

Today's Prayer:

Dear God, thank you for making everything beautiful in its time. Help me trust you as I get ready for new things and bloom with joy.

September

1
SEPTEMBER

Entering a New Season with Faith
God helps us be brave as we start new things!
(Joshua 1:9)

Little Camille looked at the big world ahead and took a deep breath. "Oh, I hope I can do it!" she whispered. Then she remembered, "Be brave, little one! God is with you!" She smiled and stepped into her new day. Just like Camille, you can try new things with God helping you be brave!

Reflection:

Can you show me how you try something new and feel brave, knowing God is with you, just like Camille?

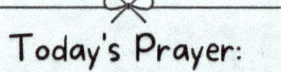

Today's Prayer:

Dear God, thank you for being with me as I try new things. Please help me be brave like Camille, knowing I can do it with your love by my side.

2
SEPTEMBER

Resting in God's Rhythm
God wants you to be happy and rest in Him, just like a cozy blanket! (Matthew 11:28)

Rianne loved to play and sing all day. But sometimes, her feet got tired and her eyes felt sleepy. She snuggled under her soft blanket and heard a gentle whisper, "Rest with Me, little one." Rianne smiled, feeling warm inside. God loves when we rest and feel happy in His cozy love!

Reflection:

When you feel tired after playing and singing, what is your favorite way to get cozy and rest with God?

Today's Prayer:

Dear God, thank you for giving me rest and cozy moments. Help me feel your love and peace when I snuggle up and rest with you.

3
SEPTEMBER

When You Feel Behind

God is always with you, holding your hand!
(Isaiah 41:10)

Rayne liked to run and play with her friends, but sometimes her steps felt slow. She worried she couldn't keep up. Then she heard a gentle voice, "I'm right here—hold My hand!" It was God! Rayne smiled and kept going. With God by her side, she knew she could do amazing things, step by step!

Reflection:

Can you show me how you keep going, holding God's hand, even when things feel slow, just like Rayne?

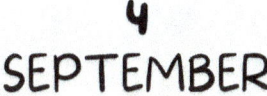

Today's Prayer:

Dear God, thank you for holding my hand and helping me keep going. Help me trust you, even when things feel slow or hard.

4
SEPTEMBER

Seeking God First

Put God first, and He will take care of you!
(Matthew 6:33)

Melissa loved to play and sing like a happy bird. One sunny day, she wanted to find the prettiest flowers. Instead of rushing, she stopped and prayed, "God, help me, please!" Then she spotted a bright, blooming garden! Melissa smiled big—when she asked God first, He showed her the way every time!

Reflection:

Can you show me how you ask God for help first, just like Melissa, and trust Him to show you the way?

Today's Prayer:

Dear God, thank you for showing me the way when I ask for your help. Please help me remember to put you first in all I do.

5
SEPTEMBER

You Are Never Alone
God is always with you, little one!
(Psalm 139:7)

Marcy was a tiny ant who loved to march and explore. One day, dark clouds rolled in, and she felt all alone. But then she remembered, "God is always with you, little one!" Marcy wiggled her antennae, smiled, and kept going. Just like Marcy, you're never alone—God walks with you every step!

Reflection:

When you feel a little scared or sad, what do you like to remember to help you feel better, just like Marcy did when the clouds rolled in?

Today's Prayer:

Dear God, thank you for being with me every step, even when I feel alone. Help me smile and keep going, knowing you are always near.

6
SEPTEMBER

Refreshed by His Presence
God loves you very much and makes you happy!
(Psalm 16:11)

Flowers twirled and giggled as sunshine warmed the garden. Ara watched them sway and felt God's love like a hug. "God loves me so much!" she smiled. When she heard birds sing and felt the breeze, her heart danced too. God's love made her feel happy and new—just like the flowers!

Reflection:

Can you think of a time when you felt really happy, like the flowers in the garden? What made your heart dance?

Today's Prayer:

Dear God, thank you for loving me and making my heart dance with happiness. Help me feel your love and joy in every moment.

7
SEPTEMBER

Trusting God's Bigger Picture
God has a great plan for you, little one!
(Jeremiah 29:11)

In a cozy garden, Claudia played among the flowers, giggling as the sun warmed her. God whispered, "I have a special plan for you, little one!" Each step she took was part of His beautiful plan. Just like a puzzle, every moment fits together perfectly. Trust Him, sweet girl—He's making something wonderful just for you!

Reflection:

Can you show me how you trust God's plan for you, knowing He's making something wonderful, just like Claudia in the garden?

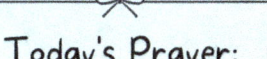

Today's Prayer:

Dear God, thank you for having a special plan for me. Help me trust you and know you're making something wonderful with my life.

8
SEPTEMBER

The Fruit of the Spirit
God gives us love, joy, and peace in our hearts!
(Galatians 5:22)

Maribel loved to play in the sunny garden, picking flowers and finding big, sweet-smelling fruits! "These are special gifts from God!" she smiled. The fruits were Love that made her hug her doll, Joy that made her giggle, and Peace that made her feel cozy inside. Every time she shared, her heart grew even happier!

Reflection:

Can you think of a time when you shared something nice with a friend or your doll? How did that make your heart feel?

Today's Prayer:

Dear God, thank you for filling my heart with love, joy, and peace. Help me share your gifts and make my heart even happier.

9
SEPTEMBER

A Faith That Grows
Faith is like a tiny seed that grows big and strong! (Matthew 17:20)

A tiny seed was planted in a sunny garden. It was small, but so special! Every day, with sunshine and rain, the seed grew bigger and stronger. Just like that seed, Hailey's faith can grow too! When we believe in God, even little faith can do amazing things. Let your faith bloom, sweet girl!

Reflection:
What do you think makes a flower grow big and strong, just like your feelings for God?

Today's Prayer:
Dear God, thank you for helping my faith grow strong like a flower. Please help me believe in you and do amazing things.

10
SEPTEMBER

Finding Joy in Serving
Helping others makes us happy!
(Acts 20:35)

Miley loved to help her friends. One day, she found a bird with a hurt wing. Gently, she helped the bird find a cozy spot to rest. When the bird smiled, Miley's heart felt warm and happy! Helping others made Miley feel joyful. Remember, sweet girl, when you help, you bring happiness to everyone!

Reflection:
Can you show me how you help someone and feel happy inside, just like Miley did with the little bird?

Today's Prayer:
Dear God, thank you for letting me help others. Please fill my heart with joy and happiness every time I serve and care for someone.

11
SEPTEMBER

God Is Your Shelter
God is like a cozy blanket that keeps you safe and warm. (Psalm 91:1)

Winona snuggled into her favorite blanket and smiled. It was soft, warm, and made her feel safe. Just like that cozy hug, God wraps you in His love every day! When you feel a little scared or lonely, remember—God is always with you, keeping you safe and happy like your blanket!

Reflection:

Can you show me how you feel safe and warm, knowing God wraps you in His love like a cozy blanket, just like Winona?

Today's Prayer:

Dear God, thank you for wrapping me in your love like a cozy blanket. Help me feel safe and happy, knowing you are always with me.

12
SEPTEMBER

The Power of Your Words
Kind words are like a warm hug!
(Proverbs 16:24)

Amara twirled in her sparkly dress, giggling with joy. She saw her friend feeling shy and whispered, "You're amazing!" Her friend smiled big and gave her a happy hug. Amara learned that kind words are like sunshine—they make hearts feel warm! Your words can spread love and joy too, sweet girl!

Reflection:

When you see your friend feeling shy, how can you use your words to make her smile like the sunshine?

Today's Prayer:

Dear God, help me use kind words to make others smile and feel loved, just like sunshine warms our hearts.

13
SEPTEMBER

Returning to God's Heart

God loves us so much and wants us to come close to Him. (1 John 4:19)

Pam skipped through a garden full of flowers, but her heart felt a little lonely. Then she heard a soft voice say, "Come close, my sweet girl. I love you so much!" Pam smiled and closed her eyes. She felt God's warm hug in her heart. He was right there, ready to love her forever and ever.

Reflection:

Can you show me how you come close to God and feel His love, just like Pam did when she felt a warm hug in her heart?

Today's Prayer:

Dear God, thank you for loving me and holding me close. Help my heart feel your warm hug and know I am never alone.

14
SEPTEMBER

Every Season Has Purpose

God made every season beautiful for us to enjoy! (Ecclesiastes 3:11)

Amber twirled through the year with joy! Spring brought tiny buds and giggles. Summer shined with splashes and sunshine. Autumn leaves crunched under her toes. Winter wrapped her in cozy hugs. God made every season just right—a special gift to enjoy, one sweet moment at a time!

Reflection:

Can you show me your favorite way to enjoy each season, knowing God made them all special, just like Amber?

Today's Prayer:

Dear God, thank you for making every season special. Help me find joy in spring, summer, autumn, and winter, knowing you made them for me.

15 SEPTEMBER

Living with Spiritual Clarity

God is light; in Him there is no darkness at all.
(1 John 1:5)

Raven loved to twirl in the sunlight, giggling as her dress sparkled bright. One day, she noticed a dark corner and felt a little shy. Then she smiled and said, "God is light!" Just like that, her heart felt warm again. God's light makes everything clear and happy—even the dark parts!

Reflection:

Can you show me how you feel happy and safe, letting God's light shine in every part of your heart, just like Raven?

$$\longrightarrow \infty \longleftarrow$$

Today's Prayer:

Dear God, thank you for shining your light in my heart. Help me feel happy and safe, knowing you make everything bright and clear.

---

16 SEPTEMBER

Letting God Carry the Load

God helps us when we feel heavy, He carries our cares! (1 Peter 5:7)

Delilah found a big toy box she couldn't lift. Her hands felt tired, and her eyes got teary. Then she remembered, "God helps me when things feel heavy!" She took a deep breath, smiled, and asked God for help. Her heart felt lighter, and she knew she wasn't alone. God loves to carry our cares!

Reflection:

Can you show me how you ask God for help when things feel heavy, just like Delilah did with her big toy box?

$$\longrightarrow \infty \longleftarrow$$

Today's Prayer:

Dear God, thank you for helping me when things feel heavy. Please carry my worries and make my heart feel light and happy.

17 SEPTEMBER

Hope in the Hidden Places

God loves me and is always with me, even when I can't see Him. (Psalm 139:7)

Faith played hide and seek and giggled behind a big tree. No one could see her, but she felt safe and loved. She smiled, thinking, "God sees me, even here!" Even when we can't see Him, God is always near. He fills every quiet, hidden place with love just for you!

Reflection:

Can you show me how you feel safe and loved, knowing God sees you and is with you, even in hidden places like Faith?

Today's Prayer:

Dear God, thank you for seeing me and loving me, even when I feel hidden. Help me feel safe and close to you everywhere I go.

•

18 SEPTEMBER

Obedient in the Unknown

Trust in God, He is always with you!
(Psalm 56:3)

Sylvie walked through a new place that felt big and dark. She held her favorite blanket tight and whispered, "I can be brave!" She remembered, "God is always with me!" Step by step, Sylvie smiled, feeling God's love light the way. Even when things feel unknown, you can trust Him too!

Reflection:

Can you show me how you take brave steps and trust God is with you, even when things feel new or a little scary, just like Sylvie?

Today's Prayer:

Dear God, thank you for being with me when things feel new or scary. Help me take brave steps, trusting your love lights my way.

19 SEPTEMBER

He Redeems Every Chapter

God loves me and makes my story beautiful!
(Psalm 147:3)

Jana loved to make colorful drawings. One day, she spilled paint everywhere! But God saw her mess and made a beautiful rainbow. Sometimes things feel messy, but God turns them into something wonderful. When you feel sad or confused, remember —God is making your story beautiful!

Reflection:

Can you show me how you trust God to make something beautiful from your messes, just like Jana's rainbow?

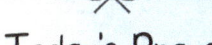

Today's Prayer:

Dear God, thank you for loving me and making my story beautiful, even when things feel messy. Help me trust you with every part of my life.

---

20 SEPTEMBER

You Are Fully Known and Loved

God loves you so much, and He knows all about you! (1 John 4:16)

Gwen had a cuddly teddy bear she loved to hug. Every time she squeezed it, she felt safe and happy. One day, she heard a soft voice say, "God loves you, Gwen, just like you love your bear!" She smiled big, knowing God knows her giggles and dreams. You are fully known and deeply loved!

Reflection:

What do you love most about your teddy bear, and how does it make you feel loved, just like how God loves you?

Today's Prayer:

Dear God, thank you for knowing me and loving me so much. Help me feel safe and happy, just like when I hug my teddy bear.

21 SEPTEMBER

Praise as a Weapon

Sing and be happy, for God loves you!
(Psalm 100:1)

Emelia loved to sing happy songs. One day, she felt a little sad, so she twirled and sang her favorite tune. With each note, her heart felt lighter! Singing to God made her smile again. Just like Emelia, when you sing and say thank you to God, joy fills your heart like sunshine!

Reflection:

Can you show me how you sing or say thank you to God, letting joy fill your heart like sunshine, just like Emelia?

Today's Prayer:

Dear God, thank you for filling my heart with joy when I sing and praise you. Help me smile and feel your love like sunshine.

---

22 SEPTEMBER

Unshaken in the Storm

God is like a big, strong rock, so we don't have to be scared! (Psalm 62:6)

Lillie heard the wind whoosh and saw the sky turn gray. A storm was coming! She held her blanket tight and whispered her special song, "God is my strong rock!" Even when thunder boomed, Lillie felt brave. Just like a big, strong rock, God keeps you safe and steady, no matter the storm!

Reflection:

Can you show me how you feel safe and brave, knowing God is your strong rock, just like Lillie in the storm?

Today's Prayer:

Dear God, thank you for being my strong rock. Help me feel safe and brave, even when storms come, knowing you are always with me.

23
SEPTEMBER

Choosing to Trust Again

Trust in God and be happy, for He loves you!
(Psalm 37:4)

Christina held her kite but felt unsure. "What if it doesn't fly?" she whispered. Mommy smiled, "Let's trust!" Christina let go, and up it soared—so high! Her giggles followed. Just like her kite, when we choose to trust God, He lifts us up with joy. He loves you so much, sweet girl!

Reflection:

Can you show me how you trust God and feel happy, just like Christina did when her kite soared high in the sky?

Today's Prayer:

Dear God, thank you for lifting me up with joy when I trust you. Help me let go of worries and feel happy in your love.

24
SEPTEMBER

Walking in Spiritual Wisdom

Walk with love and kindness, following Jesus every day! (Ephesians 5:2)

Katie loved to walk and pretend she was on a big adventure. One day, she held out her hand and said, "Jesus, walk with me!" She smiled as they skipped, shared, and gave hugs to friends. "Walk with love," Jesus whispered. And Katie did—spreading joy with every happy step!

Reflection:

Can you show me how you walk with love and kindness, just like Katie, knowing Jesus is with you on every adventure?

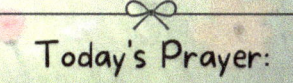

Today's Prayer:

Dear Jesus, thank you for walking with me. Help me share love and kindness with everyone I meet on my adventures with you.

25 SEPTEMBER

The Blessing of Surrender
God loves you and wants to help you be happy!
(Matthew 11:28)

Marian sat in the garden feeling a little heavy in her heart. "I want to feel happy," she whispered. Then she heard a gentle breeze say, "Let go, sweet girl. God is here to help!" Marian took a deep breath and smiled big. Her heart felt light—like a flower blooming in the sun!

Reflection:

Can you show me how you let go and feel happy, knowing God is here to help you, just like Marian in the garden?

Today's Prayer:

Dear God, thank you for helping me let go and feel happy. Please fill my heart with your love and make it light like a blooming flower.

26 SEPTEMBER

Your Life Is a Light
You are a little light that shines bright!
(Matthew 5:16)

Eina loved to giggle, share hugs, and make her friends smile. Every time she did, her heart felt like a bright light! "You shine so big!" said Mama. Eina twirled and laughed, knowing God made her to shine with love and joy. Just like a little star, she lights up the world!

Reflection:

Can you show me how you shine bright with love and joy, just like Eina, making the world a happier place?

Today's Prayer:

Dear God, thank you for making me a bright light. Help me share love and joy so I can make the world shine with your happiness.

27 SEPTEMBER

Comforted by God's Nearness

God is always with you, little one!
(Psalm 139:7)

Angela loved to explore, but one day, big shadows made her feel scared. She stopped and whispered, "God is always with me!" Then she imagined His gentle hug wrapping her tight. The shadows looked softer, and Angela smiled. She felt brave, knowing God was close and she was never alone.

Reflection:

When you feel a little scared, what do you like to imagine that makes you feel safe, just like Angela felt God's hugs?

— ✼ —

Today's Prayer:

Dear God, thank you for being with me when I feel scared. Please help me feel safe and brave, knowing your love is always near.

•

28 SEPTEMBER

Refined Through Waiting

Good Things Come To Those Who Wait.
(Psalm 27:14)

Kendall loved to explore, but sometimes she had to wait for the perfect moment. Like when she was waiting for her favorite flower to bloom, she learned that patience helps her grow, too. While she waited, God was making her strong and beautiful. Good things come to those who wait, just like Kendall!

Reflection:

Can you show me how you wait patiently and trust God to bring good things, just like Kendall waiting for her flower to bloom?

— ✼ —

Today's Prayer:

Dear God, thank you for teaching me patience. Help me trust you and wait with a happy heart, knowing good things will come.

29
SEPTEMBER

Grace for the Process
God loves you and helps you grow every day!
(Adapted from Philippians 1:6)

Eliza loved to play in the garden, but sometimes, it rained or the sun hid behind clouds. One day, a kind gardener said, "Don't worry, Eliza! God loves you and helps you grow every day!" Just like the flowers, Eliza grew stronger with each day. Remember, sweet girl, God is helping you grow too!

Reflection:

What is your favorite flower in the garden, and how do you think it feels when it rains or the sun shines?

Today's Prayer:

Dear God, thank you for loving me and helping me grow, just like flowers in the garden. Please help me trust you in every season.

30
SEPTEMBER

Celebrating God's Faithfulness
God loves you always and forever!
(Psalm 136:1)

Teagan loved to play and explore, and one day she saw a beautiful rainbow in the sky. It made her smile, remembering that God's love is bright and never fades! Just like the rainbow, God's love is always there, no matter what. So, Teagan danced and sang, feeling God's love around her every day!

Reflection:

Can you show me your biggest smile or dance, knowing God's love is always with you, just like Teagan and the rainbow?

Today's Prayer:

Dear God, thank you for your love that never fades. Help me smile and dance, knowing you are always with me, just like a rainbow.

October

Finding Peace in the Unknown

God is with you everywhere, so you don't have to be scared. (Isaiah 41:10)

Collette loved to twirl and giggle, just like a little butterfly. Sometimes, though, the world felt big and a little bit scary. When the wind blew loud or the lights got low, Collette would close her eyes and remember a special secret: God is with her everywhere she goes! That made her feel safe.

She'd take a deep breath, smile big, and twirl again. Even when things felt new or unsure, Collette knew she could feel peace inside. Just like a butterfly flying high, she was never alone—because God was always by her side!

Reflection:

Can you show me how you feel peaceful and safe, knowing God is with you everywhere, just like Collette the butterfly?

——— ✠ ———

Today's Prayer:

Dear God, thank you for being with me everywhere I go. Help me feel peaceful and safe, knowing I am never alone with you by my side.

——— ✠ ———

2
OCTOBER

You Are Chosen

You are special and loved just like a shining star!
(1 Peter 2:9)

Nala loved to twirl and laugh under the stars. One night, she heard a whisper in her heart, "You are chosen, sweet girl, just like a star!" Nala smiled big. She felt special, knowing God made her to shine bright. When she shares love and joy, she lights up the world—just by being Nala!

Reflection:

What makes you feel like a shining star, just like Nala? Is it when you twirl, or when you laugh?

Today's Prayer:

Dear God, thank you for choosing me and making me shine bright. Help me share love and joy so I can light up the world for you.

3
OCTOBER

When You Need Direction

God will show you the right way to go!
(Proverbs 3:6)

Cassandra was playing outside and came to two paths. She didn't know which one to choose. She stopped, closed her eyes, and whispered, "God, help me pick the right way!" A soft breeze tickled her cheeks, and she smiled. With God's help, Cassandra skipped down the best path, feeling safe and happy inside!

Reflection:

Can you show me how you ask God for help when you need to choose, just like Cassandra did at the two paths?

Today's Prayer:

Dear God, thank you for showing me the right way when I need help. Please guide my steps and help me feel safe and happy inside.

4
OCTOBER

Abiding Through the Chaos

God is our safe place, always with us!
(Psalm 46:1)

Flora loved to twirl and sing, but sometimes things got loud and messy. When the thunder boomed and toys tumbled, Flora felt a little scared. She closed her eyes and whispered, "God is my safe place." Wrapped in her cozy blanket, Flora felt calm. God's love was holding her tight, and her heart felt peaceful again.

Reflection:

When the noise gets loud and the toys fall down, what do you like to do to feel safe and cozy, just like Flora?

Today's Prayer:

Dear God, thank you for being my safe place when things feel loud or scary. Please hold me close and fill my heart with peace.

5
OCTOBER

The Strength to Say Yes

God helps me be brave and say 'yes' to good things! (Joshua 1:9)

Evelynn was a brave little girl who loved to explore! One sunny day, she saw her friends building a big tower with colorful blocks. "Can I help?" she asked, feeling a bit shy. Then she remembered, "God helps me be brave!" She smiled, joined in, and helped build the tallest tower ever!

Reflection:

Can you show me how you say "yes" to something new and feel brave, just like Evelynn did with her friends and the tall tower?

Today's Prayer:

Dear God, thank you for helping me be brave and say "yes" to new things. Please give me courage to join in and try good things today.

6
OCTOBER

God's Love Never Changes
God loves you, and His love is forever!
(Jeremiah 31:3)

Helena was a little star who loved to shine in the night sky. She felt so happy, knowing that God loved her very much! Even when clouds covered her, Helena felt snug in God's love, just like a warm hug. Whenever you feel wiggly or sleepy, remember: God's love is always with you, just like Helena!

Reflection:

Can you show me your happy face, knowing God's love is always with you, just like Helena the little star?

Today's Prayer:
Dear God, thank you for loving me forever. Help me feel your love like a warm hug, no matter what, just like Helena the little star.

7
OCTOBER

He Sees the Whole Picture
God sees everything and loves you very much!
(Proverbs 15:3)

Camilla lived in a beautiful garden where God watched over every flower and bee. One day, Camilla felt lost and sad, but then she heard God whisper, "I see you, my sweet one! I love you just as you are!" With a smile, Camilla felt safe and happy. Remember, God sees you and loves you always!

Reflection:

Can you show me how you feel safe and happy, knowing God sees you and loves you always, just like Camilla in the garden?

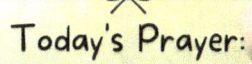

Today's Prayer:

Dear God, thank you for seeing me and loving me just as I am. Help me feel safe and happy, knowing you are always watching over me.

8
OCTOBER

A Heart Aligned with His
God loves your heart!
(1 John 4:19)

Nadia loved to dance and sing, and one day, she learned that God loved her heart just the way it was—full of joy! She imagined her heart as a bright, shining star. Every time Nadia shared her toys or smiled, her heart sparkled even more. Just like Nadia, your heart shines when you love others!

Reflection:

What makes your heart feel like a bright, shining star? Is it when you sing, dance, or share your toys with friends?

Today's Prayer:

Dear God, thank you for loving my heart and making it shine bright. Help me share your love and joy with everyone around me.

9
OCTOBER

Living with Spiritual Courage
Be strong and brave; God is with you always!
(based on Joshua 1:9)

Zuri loved to explore her big, beautiful garden. One day, she saw a spider spinning its web and felt a little scared. Then she remembered, "Be strong and brave; God is with you always!" With a big smile, Zuri took a deep breath, watched the spider, and felt God's love all around her.

Reflection:

Can you show me how you feel strong and brave, knowing God is with you always, just like Zuri in her garden?

Today's Prayer:

Dear God, thank you for being with me and helping me be strong and brave. Help me remember your love is always around me.

10
OCTOBER

The Promise of Renewal
God makes everything new and beautiful!
(Revelation 21:5)

Joelle loved to twirl through her garden in her favorite dress. One day, she felt messy and grumpy and didn't want to smile. But then she remembered, "God makes me new and beautiful!" She took a deep breath, said a little prayer, and felt His joy bloom inside. Sweet girl, God is always making you new—full of love and sparkle!

Reflection:

Can you show me how you feel new and joyful, knowing God makes you beautiful inside, just like Joelle in her garden?

～❀～

Today's Prayer:

Dear God, thank you for making me new and filling my heart with joy. Help me shine with your love and feel beautiful inside.

11
OCTOBER

Clothed in Dignity and Strength
You are special and strong, just like a beautiful flower! (Proverbs 31:25)

Adriana was like a beautiful flower, standing tall and bright in the sunshine. She knew that God made her special, just the way she is. Whenever the wind blew, she smiled and swayed, feeling strong and happy. Sweet girl, you are loved and filled with strength, just like a beautiful flower!

Reflection:

Can you show me how you feel strong and special, knowing God made you just right, like Adriana the beautiful flower?

～❀～

Today's Prayer:

Dear God, thank you for making me special and strong. Help me stand tall and shine with your love, just like a beautiful flower.

12 OCTOBER

Running the Race Well
Keep going and smile, for Jesus loves you all the while! (Hebrews 12:1)

Priscilla loved to run and play in the sunshine. One day, her friends cheered, "Let's race!" She felt a little nervous but whispered, "Jesus is with me!" With a big smile, she ran her best, cheering for others too. Sweet girl, you can run your race with joy—Jesus is always by your side!

Reflection:

When you run and play, how do you feel Knowing Jesus is cheering for you? Can you show me your biggest smile?

Today's Prayer:

Dear Jesus, thank you for cheering for me and being by my side. Help me run with joy and share my biggest smile with everyone!

---

13 OCTOBER

Trusting God When We Don't Understand
God loves you and knows the way, trust in Him every day! (Proverbs 3:5)

Addie sometimes wonders why things happen or feels confused when she doesn't understand. But God always Knows the way, even when Addie doesn't. God loves Addie and wants her to trust Him every day. When Addie feels unsure, she can talk to God and Know He will help her. God's love guides Addie and Keeps her safe, no matter what.

Reflection:

Can you show me how you trust God to help you when you feel unsure, just like Addie does when she talks to Him?

Today's Prayer:

Dear God, thank you for loving me and Knowing the way. Help me trust you and feel safe, even when I don't understand things.

14
OCTOBER

Your Faith Can Move Mountains

With a little faith, big things can happen!
(Matthew 17:20)

Via stood at the bottom of a big hill, wondering if she could climb it. She took a deep breath and remembered, "With a little faith, big things can happen!" So, step by step, she climbed with a smile. At the top, she cheered! Sweet girl, your faith can help you do amazing things, just like Via!

Reflection:

What big hill do you want to climb today, and how will you use your faith to make it happen?

Today's Prayer:

Dear God, thank you for giving me faith to do big things. Help me trust you and climb every hill with a happy heart.

15
OCTOBER

Let God Rewrite Your Story

God loves you very much and can make your heart happy! (Psalm 37:4)

Jolie felt a little sad today. Then, she heard a gentle whisper, "Let me rewrite your story!" It was God! He gave her a sprinkle of joy and a hug of hope. Her heart felt happy again! Now, when Jolie feels blue, she remembers—God makes every day a sweet, happy adventure!

Reflection:

Can you show me how you let God make your heart happy again, just like Jolie did when she felt sad?

Today's Prayer:

Dear God, thank you for making my heart happy again when I feel sad. Please fill my days with your joy and hope.

16
OCTOBER

Compassion in Action
Be kind to each other!
(Ephesians 4:32)

Chloe loved to play in her garden. One day, she saw a little bird who looked sad and hurt. Chloe gently said, "Let me help you!" She shared her soft blanket and some snacks. The bird chirped happily! Chloe smiled big, knowing that being kind and caring shows love in a special way.

Reflection:

When you see a sad bird, what kind things can you do to help it feel better, just like Chloe?

Today's Prayer:

Dear God, help me be kind and caring to others. Show me ways to help and share your love, just like Chloe did with the little bird.

17
OCTOBER

The Power of a Quiet Yes
Say 'yes' to love and kindness, just like Jesus!
(1 John 4:19)

Suzy loved to play in the garden. One day, she said "yes" to being kind and shared her toys with a friend. That little "yes" made her heart sparkle! Each time Suzy chose love, the world felt brighter. Just like Jesus, we can say "yes" to kindness and fill the day with joy!

Reflection:

Can you show me how you say "yes" to kindness and make your heart sparkle, just like Suzy did in the garden?

Today's Prayer:

Dear God, help me say "yes" to kindness and love. Make my heart sparkle and fill my day with your joy, just like Suzy's.

18 OCTOBER

Celebrating God's Goodness

God made everything good and loves us so much!
(Genesis 1:31)

Sue looked at the bright sun, pretty flowers, and fluffy clouds and smiled big. "God made all this!" she giggled. From sweet strawberries to singing birds, everything shows how good God is. When Sue claps and twirls, she's saying, "Thank You, God!" Let's celebrate—God is so good!

Reflection:

Can you show me how you celebrate and say "Thank You, God!" for all the good things He made, just like Sue?

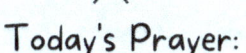

Today's Prayer:

Dear God, thank you for all the good things you made. Help me celebrate and say "Thank You!" with a happy heart, just like Sue.

---

19 OCTOBER

Your Voice Matters

Your voice is special and sweet, just like you!
(Psalm 34:1)

Mariah loved to sing to her dolls, her teddy bear, and even her puppy! One day, she learned a special secret—her voice is like a pretty flower that makes hearts happy. God gave Mariah her sweet voice on purpose! Every time she sings or speaks with love, her voice shines bright—just like her!

Reflection:

What do you like to sing to your dolls and teddy bear that makes them smile just like your voice does?

Today's Prayer:

Dear God, thank you for my special voice. Help me use it to share love and make hearts happy, just like a pretty flower.

20 OCTOBER

He Delights in You

You are so special to God, and He loves you so much! (Zephaniah 3:17)

Patty loved to twirl and dance every day, giggling with joy! One sunny morning, God looked down and smiled, saying, "Patty, you are so special! I love you just the way you are!" Patty felt warm inside, knowing God was always with her, cheering her on. Every time she danced, it made God happy!

Reflection:

When you twirl and dance, how does it make your heart feel knowing that God loves to see you happy?

Today's Prayer:

Dear God, thank you for loving me and cheering me on. Help my heart feel happy and special, knowing you delight in me.

---

21 OCTOBER

Pursuing God Over Perfection

God loves you just as you are!
(1 John 3:1)

Viv loved to dance and play, but sometimes she wanted everything to be perfect. One day, her bunny friend said, "Viv, God loves you just as you are!" Viv smiled and twirled, realizing that having fun was much better than being perfect. She danced with her friends, knowing they were all loved just the way they were.

Reflection:

Can you show me how you have fun and feel loved, knowing God loves you just as you are, just like Viv?

Today's Prayer:

Dear God, thank you for loving me just as I am. Help me have fun and feel your love, knowing I don't have to be perfect.

22 OCTOBER

Brave Steps of Obedience

Be strong and brave; God is always with you!
(Joshua 1:9)

Margo wanted to climb a big hill, but it looked so tall! She remembered what God said: "Be strong and brave; God is always with you!" So, Margo took a deep breath and took her first step. Step by step, she climbed higher, feeling God cheering her on. When she reached the top, she smiled, knowing bravery comes from trusting God!

Reflection:

Can you show me how you take brave steps, trusting God is with you, just like Margo climbing her big hill?

Today's Prayer:

Dear God, thank you for being with me as I take brave steps. Help me trust you and feel strong, knowing you are always by my side.

---

23 OCTOBER

Faith that Overflows

God's love is like a big, warm hug that never stops! (Romans 5:5)

Yesha loved big, warm hugs! One day, she learned God's love is just like that—big and never-ending! Whether happy, sad, or sleepy, God's love wrapped around her like a fluffy blanket. Every smile and share felt like a hug from her heart. Yesha danced with joy, knowing His hugs were always there!

Reflection:

Can you show me how you feel God's big, warm hug around you, just like Yesha, no matter how you feel?

Today's Prayer:

Dear God, thank you for your big, warm love that hugs me always. Help me feel your love and share it with others every day.

24 OCTOBER

Finding Comfort in Scripture
God loves you and takes care of you.
(Psalm 23:1)

Brooke loved to play in the cozy forest, knowing her big, gentle friend, God, watched over her. One day, she found a soft patch of grass and whispered, "God loves me and takes care of me." As the sun warmed her skin, she smiled, feeling safe and loved. Just like Brooke, God is always with you!

Reflection:

Can you show me how you feel safe and loved, knowing God takes care of you, just like Brooke in the cozy forest?

Today's Prayer:

Dear God, thank you for loving me and taking care of me. Help me feel safe and happy, knowing you are always with me, just like Brooke.

---

25 OCTOBER

Strength for the Surrender
God is my helper; I can be strong and brave!
(Psalm 118:7)

Karina wanted to try a big jump, but it felt a little scary. She took a deep breath and whispered, "God is my helper—I can be strong and brave!" With a giggle and a hop, she jumped high and landed with a smile. Just like Karina, you can try new things with God's strength in your heart!

Reflection:

Can you show me how you try something new and feel strong and brave, knowing God is your helper, just like Karina?

Today's Prayer:

Dear God, thank you for being my helper. Help me feel strong and brave when I try new things, just like Karina.

26 OCTOBER

You Were Made for This Season

God made you special for this time, just like the flowers bloom in spring! (Ecclesiastes 3:1)

Kira twirled in the sunshine and giggled in the rain. She looked around and thought, "God made me for this!" Just like spring flowers, Kira was made to shine and share joy. Her hugs, laughs, and love made the world brighter. Sweet girl, you were made for this season—full of fun, love, and God's big plan for you!

Reflection:

Can you show me how you shine and share joy, knowing God made you special for this season, just like Kira?

Today's Prayer:

Dear God, thank you for making me special for this season. Help me shine and share joy, just like flowers blooming in spring.

---

27 OCTOBER

The Anchor of God's Word

God's words are like a strong anchor that keeps us safe! (Hebrews 6:19)

Amanda had a little boat that bobbed on the water. One breezy day, the waves went *splash splash!* Amanda held her teddy and said, "It's okay!" Her boat had a strong anchor. It kept her safe and still. God's words are just like that anchor—they help our hearts feel safe and happy too. God keeps us safe and sound!

Reflection:

Can you show me how you feel safe and happy, knowing God's words are like a strong anchor, just like Amanda in her boat?

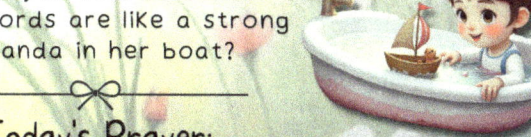

Today's Prayer:

Dear God, thank you for your words that keep me safe and happy. Help my heart feel anchored and strong, just like Amanda's boat.

28
OCTOBER

Trusting Him, Even in Silence
Even when I can't see Him, God is always with me!
(Psalm 139:7)

Bree held her bunny tight as they played in the meadow. One day, Bunny couldn't find her squirrel friend and felt a little scared. Bree whispered, "Even when I can't see Him, God is always with me!" Just then—rustle, rustle—the squirrel popped out! Bree giggled, knowing love is always near, even when it's quiet.

Reflection:

Can you show me how you trust God is with you, even when you can't see Him, just like Bree and her bunny?

Today's Prayer:

Dear God, thank you for being with me, even when I can't see you. Help me trust your love is always near, just like Bree did.

29
OCTOBER

Living Gratefully
Give thanks for everything!
(1 Thessalonians 5:18)

Keyna loved playing in her garden, dancing with butterflies and listening to the birds. One sunny day, she found a shiny, red apple. "Thank you, God, for my yummy apple!" she giggled. She remembered to say thank you for her family, friends, and even her teddy bear. Just like Keyna, we can always say thank you!

Reflection:

Can you show me how you say "thank you" for the good things God gives you, just like Keyna with her apple?

Today's Prayer:

Dear God, thank you for all the good things you give me. Help me remember to say "thank you" with a happy heart, just like Keyna.

30 OCTOBER

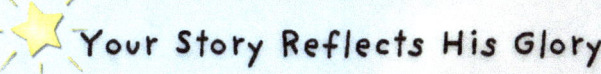

Your Story Reflects His Glory

You are special, just like a shining star!
(Matthew 5:16)

In the bright sky, many twinkling stars shined in their own special way, just like you, Jennie! God made you to sparkle and shine. When you share your smiles and kindness, you light up the world, just like the stars light up the night. So, whenever you play or laugh, remember, you reflect God's glory!

Reflection:

Jennie, when you smile and play, how do you think you can make the world shine brighter, just like the twinkling stars in the sky?

Today's Prayer:

Dear God, thank you for making me shine bright like a star. Help me share smiles and kindness to light up the world for you.

---

31 OCTOBER

Walking in the Light

Walk in the light and be happy!
(John 8:12)

Brittney loved to play in the sunshine. One day, she discovered a magical path filled with sparkly lights. Every time she stepped on the bright stones, she giggled and danced, feeling so happy! "This is what it means to walk in the light!" she said. Remember, sweet one, walk in love and kindness, and feel joy in your heart!

Reflection:

Can you show me how you walk in love and kindness, feeling joy in your heart, just like Brittney on her sparkly path?

Today's Prayer:

Dear God, thank you for showing me how to walk in your light. Help me share love and kindness and fill my heart with joy each day.

November

1
NOVEMBER

Gratitude in Every Circumstance

Give thanks to God for everything!
(1 Thessalonians 5:18)

Beth was a joyful little girl who loved the sunshine and chasing butterflies. One day, dark clouds came, and the rain made her feel a little gloomy. But Beth took a deep breath and said, "Thank you, God, for the rain!" Soon, puddles sparkled, and her giggles returned. Rainy days can bring joy too!

Reflection:

Can you show me how you say "thank you" to God, even on rainy days, just like Beth did when she saw the puddles sparkle?

Today's Prayer:

Dear God, thank you for sunshine and rain. Help me find joy and say "thank you" in every moment, just like Beth.

2
NOVEMBER

He is Faithful Still

God loves you all the time!
(1 John 4:16)

Cristie loved to twirl in the garden and chase butterflies. One day, the sky turned gray and the wind blew. She felt a little sad. But then she smiled and whispered, "God loves me all the time!" Even when it rained, Cristie danced in puddles, knowing God's love never goes away—rain or shine!

Reflection:

When you dance in the rain or chase butterflies, how do you feel God's love around you?

Today's Prayer:

Dear God, thank you for loving me all the time, rain or shine. Help me feel your love and dance with joy, no matter the weather.

3 NOVEMBER

Strength in Surrender
God is my helper; I can be brave and strong!
(Psalm 118:14)

Aurelia was a brave little girl who loved to climb just like Bella Bear in her favorite story. One day, the hill looked extra tall, and her friend felt nervous too. Aurelia took a deep breath and said, "Let's be brave together!" As they climbed, she smiled—God helps us do big things, even when we feel small!

Reflection:

What is something big you can do today, just like Aurelia and Bella Bear, that makes you feel brave even if it feels a little scary?

Today's Prayer:

Dear God, thank you for helping me be brave and strong. Please help me do big things, even when I feel small or scared.

---

4 NOVEMBER

The Power of Remembering
God loves when we remember the good things He has done! (Psalm 103:2)

Julienne loved to play in her sunny garden. One day, she found shiny little stones. Each one made her smile—like flowers blooming, her puppy's silly tricks, and yummy cookies from Mom. As she remembered, her heart felt happy! Just like Julienne, we can thank God for all the good things He gives!

Reflection:

Can you show me how you remember and thank God for the good things He gives you, just like Julienne with her shiny stones?

Today's Prayer:

Dear God, thank you for all the good things you give me. Help me remember your gifts and say thank you with a happy heart.

5 NOVEMBER

Walking Through Grief with God

God is with you when you are sad, holding your hand and making you feel better. (Psalm 34:18)

Ysabel was a sweet girl who loved sunny days. But one morning, the sky was gray, and she felt a little sad. She sat by her window and whispered, "God, are You with me?" A warm feeling filled her heart. God was holding her hand! Even on rainy days, God stays close, helping us feel safe and loved.

Reflection:

Can you show me how you feel safe and loved, Knowing God holds your hand when you feel sad, just like Ysabel?

Today's Prayer:

Dear God, thank you for holding my hand and loving me when I feel sad. Help me feel safe and better, Knowing you are always close.

---

6 NOVEMBER

Rest for the Weary

Come to me, all you who are tired, and I will give you rest. (Matthew 11:28)

Allie loved to run, play, and giggle all day long. But one afternoon, her legs felt wobbly and her eyes droopy. She sat down and heard a gentle whisper in her heart, "It's okay to rest." Allie snuggled into her blanket, took a deep breath, and smiled. God gives rest when we're tired—and that's a sweet gift!

Reflection:

Can you show me how you rest and feel cozy, Knowing God gives you rest when you're tired, just like Allie?

Today's Prayer:

Dear God, thank you for giving me rest when I'm tired. Help me feel cozy and safe in your love, just like Allie.

7
NOVEMBER

Finding Contentment in Christ

Jesus loves me and gives me everything I need. (Philippians 4:19)

Madeline had a big heart and loved playing with her toys. One sunny day, she smiled and said, "Jesus gives me everything I need!" When she felt a little sad or wanted more, she took a deep breath and whispered, "Thank you, Jesus!" God's love filled her heart with joy, and that was enough!

Reflection:

Can you show me how you feel happy and thankful, knowing Jesus gives you everything you need, just like Madeline?

Today's Prayer:

Dear Jesus, thank you for giving me all I need. Help my heart feel happy and thankful, just like Madeline.

8
NOVEMBER

You Are Held

You are always in God's arms, sweet girl! (Isaiah 41:10)

Jackie loved to play and explore. One day, while climbing, she felt a little scared. But then she remembered something special: "You are always in God's arms, sweet girl!" She took a deep breath and smiled. With God holding her tight, she jumped back into her adventure, safe and loved!

Reflection:

Can you show me how you feel safe and loved, knowing you are always in God's arms, just like Jackie?

Today's Prayer:

Dear God, thank you for holding me in your arms. Help me feel safe and loved, knowing you are always with me, just like Jackie.

9
NOVEMBER

A Spirit of Thanksgiving

Give thanks to the Lord, for He is good!
(Psalm 136:1)

Maci loved to hop and explore the sunny garden. One day, she found a shiny red apple under a tree. She held it close and said, "Thank you, God, for this yummy treat!" Every time she saw pretty flowers or heard bird songs, she smiled and said, "Thank you, God!" Let's be thankful every day, just like Maci!

Reflection:

What makes you feel happy like Maci when you explore outside? Can you think of something you want to say "thank you" for today?

———————✄———————

Today's Prayer:

Dear God, thank you for all the good things you give me. Help me have a thankful heart and remember to say "thank you" every day.

───────────●───────────

10
NOVEMBER

When God Feels Distant

God is always with us, even when we can't see Him. (Psalm 139:7)

Selena loved to play, but sometimes she felt a little lonely. One day, her friend, the butterfly, whispered, "Remember, Selena, God is always with you, even when you can't see Him!" Selena smiled, imagining God holding her hand. She twirled and laughed, knowing she was never alone, because God was always with her.

Reflection:

Can you show me how you feel happy and safe, knowing God is always with you, just like Selena and her butterfly friend?

———————✄———————

Today's Prayer:

Dear God, thank you for being with me, even when I can't see you. Help me feel happy and safe, knowing I am never alone.

11
NOVEMBER

Peace That Passes Understanding
God gives us peace in our hearts, even when we are scared. (Philippians 4:7)

Dulce loved to play, but sometimes loud noises and big shadows made her feel scared. One day, she remembered a special promise from God: "He gives us peace in our hearts, even when we are scared." Dulce took a deep breath, imagining a sunny meadow, and felt safe and happy, knowing God's peace was always with her.

Reflection:

Can you show me how you feel peaceful and safe, knowing God gives you peace in your heart, just like Dulce?

Today's Prayer:

Dear God, thank you for giving me peace in my heart. Help me feel safe and happy, even when things are loud or scary, just like Dulce.

12
NOVEMBER

He Restores What Was Broken
God helps fix things that are broken and makes us happy again! (Psalm 147:3)

Mae felt sad when her favorite doll broke her arm. But then, she remembered that God could help fix things! Just like that, God helped Mae feel better, making her smile again. Whenever something feels broken or wrong, God is always there to help and make it right, bringing joy back into our hearts!

Reflection:

Can you show me how you feel happy again, knowing God helps fix what's broken, just like Mae and her doll?

Today's Prayer:

Dear God, thank you for helping me feel happy again when things are broken. Please fix my heart and bring back my smile, just like Mae.

13 NOVEMBER

You Are Called and Equipped

You are special and loved by God, just like the stars in the sky! (Psalm 139:14)

Gigi looked up at the twinkling stars, each one shining just for her. "I am special, just like these stars!" she thought. God made Gigi unique and filled her with love and joy. Just like the stars, Gigi has a special purpose. So, whenever you smile or play, remember you are called and equipped by God! Shine bright, sweet Gigi!

Reflection:

Can you show me how you shine bright and feel special, knowing God made you unique, just like Gigi and the stars?

———✄———

Today's Prayer:

Dear God, thank you for making me special and giving me a purpose. Help me shine bright and share your love, just like the stars.

---

14 NOVEMBER

Hope That Anchors

God gives us hope, like an anchor that keeps us safe! (Hebrews 6:19)

Cecilia loved to play near the big, blue sea, where she imagined sailing in a boat named Hope. Sometimes the waves were big, and the wind was strong, but Cecilia knew she was safe because God was her anchor. Just like Hope, God holds us tight and keeps us safe, giving us hope that anchors our hearts!

Reflection:

What makes you feel safe like an anchor when you play by the big, blue sea?

———✄———

Today's Prayer:

Dear God, thank you for being my anchor and keeping me safe. Help my heart feel strong and full of hope, just like Cecilia by the sea.

15 NOVEMBER

A Grateful Heart is a Strong Heart

Thank you, God, for all I have!
(1 Thessalonians 5:18)"

Shannon loved playing in the sunny garden, where she saw flowers, trees, and her cozy home. One day, the wind blew hard, but Shannon remembered all the good things she had. She smiled and said, "Thank you, God!" Her heart felt strong and full of joy. A grateful heart makes us brave and happy, just like Shannon!

Reflection:

What is something in your garden, like flowers or trees, that makes you happy and that you can say "thank you" for?

———— ✿ ————

Today's Prayer:

Dear God, thank you for flowers, trees, and my cozy home. Fill my heart with joy and help me always be grateful, just like Shannon.

---

16 NOVEMBER

Letting Go of What No Longer Serves

Let go and be happy, for God loves you!
(Psalm 37:5)

Aileen loved to play in the bright garden, where the butterfly danced in the sun. One day, Aileen saw the butterfly let go of old, tired leaves. "Let go and be happy," the butterfly whispered. Aileen smiled and thought, "I can be free too!" With a happy heart, she twirled and danced, knowing God loves her always.

Reflection:

Can you show me how you let go and feel free and happy, knowing God loves you, just like Aileen and the butterfly?

———— ✿ ————

Today's Prayer:

Dear God, thank you for loving me and helping me let go. Fill my heart with freedom and joy, just like Aileen and the butterfly.

17
NOVEMBER

Faith in the Fire
God is with you when you are scared, just like a big hug! (Isaiah 43:2)

Judith felt a little scared when she saw big, bright flames in a storybook. But then, her favorite teddy bear whispered, "Don't worry, Judith! God is with you like a big hug, even in scary times!" Judith smiled, imagining God wrapping her in a warm, cozy hug. She knew His love would always make her feel safe!

Reflection:

What would you like to tell your favorite teddy bear when you feel a little scared, just like Judith did?

Today's Prayer:

Dear God, thank you for being with me when I feel scared. Help me feel your warm hug and know your love keeps me safe, just like Judith.

18
NOVEMBER

The Blessing of Today
Every day is a gift from God, full of love and joy! (Psalm 118:24)

Cameron woke up with a big smile, excited for the new day. She found a special gift waiting—today! God filled her day with sunshine, giggles, and love. "Today is so special!" she said, dancing around. As she played, Cameron felt God's love in the flowers and the birds. Just like Cameron, remember that each day is a beautiful gift from God!

Reflection:

What is something special you saw or heard today that made you smile, just like Cameron?

Today's Prayer:

Dear God, thank you for the gift of today. Help me see your love in every smile, flower, and song, just like Cameron.

19
NOVEMBER

Preparing Your Heart for Worship

"Let's love God with our hearts and sing happy songs to Him! (Psalm 100:2)

Maris loved to sing, especially when the sun was shining. One day, she learned that singing with a happy heart made her feel close to God. She clapped her hands, twirled, and sang songs full of love. "Let's sing for God!" she giggled. Just like Maris, when we sing with joy, we share our love with God!

Reflection:

Can you show me how you sing and clap with a happy heart, sharing your love with God, just like Maris?

Today's Prayer:

Dear God, thank you for happy songs and sunshine. Help me sing and clap with love, sharing my joy with you, just like Maris.

20
NOVEMBER

Trust That Triumphs

Trust in God, He makes you brave!
(Psalm 56:3)

Clarisse felt a little scared walking through the big, dark woods. But then she remembered her mommy's words: "Trust in God, He makes you brave!" So, Clarisse took a deep breath and stepped forward. With each step, she felt stronger. Just like Clarisse, we can trust God to help us be brave when we're scared!

Reflection:

Can you show me how you trust God and feel brave, even when you're scared, just like Clarisse in the woods?

Today's Prayer:

Dear God, thank you for helping us when we feel scared. We trust in you, for you make us brave and strong, just like brave little Clarisse in the dark woods.

21
NOVEMBER

Thankfulness as Worship
Thank you, God, for all your love!
(1 Chronicles 16:34)

Elaine loved playing with her toys and smiling at the sunshine. One day, she looked up at the sky and whispered, "Thank you, God, for all your love!" She twirled like the flowers in the breeze, her heart full of joy. Saying thank you made her feel close to God—just like a big hug of love!

Reflection:

Can you show me how you say "thank you" to God and feel close to Him, just like Elaine twirling in the sunshine?

Today's Prayer:

Dear God, thank you for your love and sunshine. Help me say "thank you" and feel close to you, just like Elaine in the breeze.

22
NOVEMBER

God's Goodness Never Fails
God is good and loves us always!
(Psalm 136:1)

Juliet loved to dance in the flowers and giggle with her friends. One day, she heard a whisper, "God is good and loves you always!" Her heart felt warm, like sunshine on her face. Even when the rain came, Juliet splashed in puddles, knowing God's goodness was with her every day.

Reflection:

Can you show me how you feel God's goodness and love, even on rainy days, just like Juliet splashing in puddles?

Today's Prayer:

Dear God, thank you for your goodness and love, even on rainy days. Help me feel your warmth and joy, just like Juliet.

23
NOVEMBER

Celebrating Small Things
Every good gift is from God!
(James 1:17)

Charmie loved flowers and sunshine. One day, she found a tiny red ladybug on a leaf. "What a sweet gift from God!" she giggled. Charmie twirled with joy, thankful for the ladybug, the butterflies, and the warm breeze. Just like Charmie, we can celebrate all the small things God gives us each day!

Reflection:

What small thing made you smile today, just like Charmie with her ladybug? Can you think of something in nature that brings you joy?

Today's Prayer:

Dear God, thank you for all the small gifts you give me. Help me notice and celebrate your blessings, just like Charmie and her ladybug.

24
NOVEMBER

His Mercy Is New Today
God's love is fresh and new every morning!
(Lamentations 3:22-23)

Tessa twirled through the garden, her toes tickled by dewy grass. Every morning felt like a hug from God—fresh and full of love! When Tessa felt grumpy or sad, she smiled, remembering God gives new mercy each day. Just like a blooming flower, she could start again with joy!

Reflection:

Can you show me how you start fresh and smile, knowing God's love is new every morning, just like Tessa in the garden?

Today's Prayer:

Dear God, thank you for your new love every morning. Help me start fresh and smile with joy, just like Tessa in the garden.

25
NOVEMBER

Rooted in Gratitude
Thank you, God, for everything!
(1 Thessalonians 5:18)

Nadine saw the sun peek through the clouds. "Thank you, God, for the sunshine!" she smiled. A bright yellow canary flew by, singing sweetly. "Thank you, God, for the canary!" she giggled. With every flower, breeze, and giggle, Nadine's heart grew thankful. Just like Nadine, we can thank God for everything, big or small!

Reflection:

What is something outside that makes you smile? Can you say thank you for it, just like Nadine did for the sun and the canary?

Today's Prayer:

Dear God, thank you for sunshine, birds, and all the little things that make me smile. Help my heart stay thankful like Nadine's.

26
NOVEMBER

Overflowing with Thanksgiving
Thank you, God, for all your gifts!
(1 Thessalonians 5:18)

Jenny skipped through the sunny garden, spotting bright flowers and yummy carrots. "Thank you, God, for all your gifts!" she sang. A butterfly fluttered by, and Jenny twirled with joy. Whether it's a warm hug or tasty snack, Jenny's heart was full. Just like Jenny, we can say thank you too!

Reflection:

What is something that makes you feel happy and thankful, just like Jenny in the sunny garden?

Today's Prayer:

Dear God, thank you for all your gifts that make me happy. Help me remember to say thank you and share my joy, just like Jenny.

27
NOVEMBER

God's Faithfulness Through Generations

God loves us forever and ever!
(Psalm 100:5)

Samara skipped through the meadow, hearing birds sing and flowers sway. "God takes care of you," they seemed to say. She smiled, knowing God loved her today, tomorrow, and forever. Just like the happy animals, Samara shared God's love with hugs and giggles, feeling safe in His forever care.

Reflection:

Can you show me how you feel safe and loved, knowing God cares for you forever, just like Samara in the meadow?

Today's Prayer:

Dear God, thank you for loving me forever and taking care of me. Help me feel safe and share your love with hugs and smiles.

●

28
NOVEMBER

Blessed to Be a Blessing

You are so special, and God loves you!
(Genesis 12:2)

Honey twirled through the garden, her laughter floating like butterflies. God whispered, "You are special, and I love you!" Honey felt warm and happy. She shared her toys and hugs, spreading joy like sunshine. Just like Honey, you are a sweet blessing, made to share love with the world!

Reflection:

What makes you feel happy to share your toys and hugs with your friends, just like Honey did in the garden?

Today's Prayer:

Dear God, thank you for loving me and making me a blessing. Help me share my toys and hugs to spread your joy to others.

29
NOVEMBER

Finding Joy in Simplicity
Joy is finding happiness in small things!
(Psalm 118:24)

Melody danced with butterflies and giggled at ants marching in a line. She picked up shiny rocks and smiled at the bird's sweet song. "Joy is in the little things!" she sang. Like hugs, flowers, or laughter, joy was everywhere! Just like Melody, you can find joy in every tiny, happy moment!

Reflection:

Can you show me how you find joy in little things, like hugs or flowers, just like Melody dancing with butterflies?

Today's Prayer:

Dear God, thank you for filling my days with little joys. Help me find happiness in small things, just like Melody, and share my joy with others.

30
NOVEMBER

Grace to End the Month Well
God loves you, and He helps you every day!
(Psalm 136:1)

Daphney twirled in the garden, feeling the sunshine on her cheeks. "God loves me!" she giggled. Each breeze felt like a hug from God. As the month ended, Daphney smiled, remembering both sunny and rainy days. God helped her through them all! Just like Daphney, you can bloom with His love every day!

Reflection:

Can you show me how you bloom with God's love, smiling through sunny and rainy days, just like Daphney?

Today's Prayer:

Dear God, thank you for loving me through sunny and rainy days. Help me bloom with your love and smile, just like Daphney.

December

Preparing Him Room

Let's make room in our hearts for Jesus to come and be with us! (Luke 2:7)

Elianna saw her cozy blanket and soft toys cuddled close on the floor. She smiled and picked up her teddy. "I'll save a spot for Jesus!" she whispered, making a warm, snuggly space just for Him. Then Elianna shared her toys, gave big hugs, and sang a happy song. Her heart felt full and bright! Every time she shared love and kindness, Jesus filled her with joy and peace. Just like Elianna, we can make room for Jesus too— by loving, sharing, and caring every day!

Reflection:

Can you show me how you make room for Jesus in your heart by sharing, loving, and caring, just like Elianna?

Today's Prayer:

Dear Jesus, help me make room in my heart for you. Fill me with your love as I share, care, and show kindness every day.

2
DECEMBER

Peace in the Waiting
God is with you while you wait,
be happy and calm! (Isaiah 41:10)

Dara wanted to play with her friend, but she had to wait. She sat in the grass and whispered, "God is with me!" A butterfly flew by, and Dara smiled. She twirled and giggled, feeling calm inside. Waiting wasn't so hard with God near. Just like Dara, you can feel happy and peaceful while you wait!

Reflection:

Can you show me how you feel happy and calm while you wait, knowing God is with you, just like Dara?

Today's Prayer:

Dear God, thank you for being with me while I wait. Help me feel happy and calm, knowing you are always near, just like Dara.

3
DECEMBER

The Gift of Hope
God gives us hope, and it shines
like a bright light! (Romans 15:13)

Danielle skipped through the garden, singing a happy tune. She saw a droopy flower and gently smiled. "God gives us hope, like sunshine!" she said. The flower perked up, and so did Danielle's heart. Just like Danielle, you can shine bright with hope and share God's joy with everyone around!

Reflection:

When you see a flower in the garden, how can you share your happy song and help it smile like Danielle did?

Today's Prayer:

Dear God, thank you for giving me hope and joy. Help me share your light and make others smile, just like Danielle in the garden.

4
DECEMBER

Emmanuel—God With Us
God is always with us, like a cozy hug!
(Matthew 1:23)

Cathy loved to laugh, play, and snuggle her teddy bear. One quiet day, she felt a little sad. But then she smiled and said, "God is with me, like a cozy hug!" She closed her eyes and felt His love all around. Cathy twirled with joy, knowing she was never alone—God was always right there!

Reflection:

Can you think of a time when you felt a little sad? What makes you feel cozy and happy, just like when God is with you?

─── ✄ ───

Today's Prayer:

Dear God, thank you for being with me like a cozy hug. Help me feel your love and joy, even when I feel a little sad, just like Cathy.

5
DECEMBER

Letting God Interrupt Your Plans
Trust in the Lord with all your heart!
(Proverbs 3:5)

Avery loved building the tallest tower with her blocks. She had big plans! But then her friend wanted to play something else. Avery felt a little upset, but she took a deep breath and trusted God. She shared her blocks—and guess what? They built the biggest tower together with happy hearts!

Reflection:

Can you show me how you trust God and share, even when your plans change, just like Avery with her blocks?

─── ✄ ───

Today's Prayer:

Dear God, help me trust you and share with others, even when my plans change. Fill my heart with joy, just like Avery's.

6
DECEMBER

The Light Has Come
Jesus is the light that makes us happy!
(John 8:12)

Heidi saw a bright light shining in the sky. "Look, look!" she giggled. It was Jesus, the special light that makes everyone happy! When Jesus shines in our hearts, we feel joyful and kind, just like playing outside on sunny days. Whenever you feel that glow, remember, Jesus is the light that fills us with happiness!

Reflection:

Can you show me your happy face, knowing Jesus is the light that fills your heart with joy, just like Heidi?

———————— ✺ ————————

Today's Prayer:

Dear Jesus, thank you for being my special light. Fill my heart with joy and kindness, so I can shine bright and make others happy too.

———————————————— • ————————————————

7
DECEMBER

He Fulfills His Promises
God always keeps His promises, like a good friend! (Psalm 145:13)

Miranda loved to play in the garden, always trusting that God would keep His promises. One sunny day, she wanted to find a shiny red berry. "I trust you, God!" she giggled. Miranda searched high and low, and guess what? She found it! Just like Miranda, remember, God always keeps His promises, just like a good friend!

Reflection:

Can you show me how you trust God to keep His promises, just like Miranda searching for her shiny red berry?

———————— ✺ ————————

Today's Prayer:

Dear God, thank you for always keeping your promises. Help me trust you and remember you are a good friend, just like Miranda did.

8
DECEMBER

A Season of Surrender
Trust in God, He loves you so!
(Proverbs 3:5)

Michelle tiptoed through the garden, watching a butterfly twirl in the air. Sometimes, she felt a little scared to try new things. Then she remembered, "Trust in God, He loves you so!" Michelle took a deep breath, smiled big, and danced like the butterfly. God helped her feel brave and free!

Reflection:

When you see a butterfly dancing in the air, do you think it feels happy? What makes you feel brave, just like Michelle?

Today's Prayer:

Dear God, thank you for loving me and helping me feel brave. Help me trust you and try new things, just like Michelle and the butterfly.

9
DECEMBER

Welcoming Wonder
Look at the beautiful world God made; it's full of wonder! (Psalm 104:24)

Princess skipped through the colorful world around her. She saw trees dancing, flowers smiling, and birds singing sweet songs. "Wow!" she giggled. Every sound and sparkle felt like a gift from God. Princess twirled with joy, remembering the world is full of wonder—just for her!

Reflection:

What makes you feel happy like Princess when you see or hear something special in the world around you?

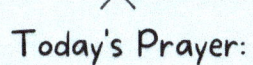

Today's Prayer:

Dear God, thank you for the wonder and beauty all around me. Help me notice your gifts and feel joy, just like Princess.

10
DECEMBER

Trusting Through Transition
God is with you wherever you go!
(Joshua 1:9)

Estelle felt a little nervous about going somewhere new. She held her teddy tight and whispered, "God is with me wherever I go!" With a big breath and a brave heart, Estelle smiled and took a step. Just like Estelle, you can feel safe and happy, knowing God goes with you too!

Reflection:

Can you show me how you feel safe and brave, knowing God goes with you everywhere, just like Estelle?

Today's Prayer:

Dear God, thank you for going with me everywhere I go. Help me feel safe and brave, just like Estelle, knowing you are always by my side.

11
DECEMBER

The Strength of a Willing Heart
God loves when you help others and try your best! (Colossians 3:23)

Ophelia loved to help! One sunny day, she saw her friend feeling sad. Ophelia picked some flowers and shared a big hug. Her heart felt warm and happy! Just like Ophelia, when you help others and try your best, you shine bright and make God smile. A willing heart is a strong heart!

Reflection:

Can you show me how you help others and shine bright, just like Ophelia, making God smile with your willing heart?

Today's Prayer:

Dear God, thank you for giving me a willing heart. Help me help others and shine bright, making you smile, just like Ophelia.

12
DECEMBER

Heaven's Perspective
God loves you and wants you to be happy every day! (John 3:16)

Francesca loved to imagine the sky filled with fluffy clouds and happy angels. She giggled and twirled, feeling God's love like sunshine on her cheeks. When she shared or gave hugs, she knew she made God smile. You are His treasure too—so loved, so special, and full of joy from heaven!

Reflection:

Can you show me how you feel special and joyful, knowing God loves you so much, just like Francesca in the sunshine?

Today's Prayer:

Dear God, thank you for loving me and making me your special treasure. Fill my heart with joy and help me share your love every day.

13
DECEMBER

Finding Joy in Christ
Jesus makes us smile and happy!
(John 15:11)

Martha loved to giggle and play with her favorite toys. One day, she heard a sweet story about Jesus and how knowing Him fills our hearts with joy. Martha twirled with a big smile, feeling His love like sunshine inside. Just like Martha, you can find joy in Jesus every day!

Reflection:

Can you show me your biggest smile, knowing Jesus fills your heart with joy, just like Martha?

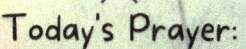

Today's Prayer:

Dear Jesus, thank you for filling my heart with joy and making me smile. Help me share your happiness with others, just like Martha.

14
DECEMBER

Holding Space for Silence
Be still and listen; God loves you so much.
(Psalm 46:10)

Lorelei loved to giggle and run, but sometimes her heart felt a little jumbled. One sunny day, she sat under her favorite tree, closed her eyes, and took a deep breath. In the quiet, Lorelei felt God's love like a warm hug. When you're still, like Lorelei, you can feel God's love too!

Reflection:

Can you show me how you sit still and feel God's love, just like Lorelei under her favorite tree?

Today's Prayer:

Dear God, thank you for loving me so much. Help me be still and feel your love, just like Lorelei under her favorite tree.

15
DECEMBER

Receiving God's Peace
God gives us peace like a soft hug.
(Philippians 4:7)

Mariana felt a little flutter in her heart while playing in the garden. She stopped, closed her eyes, and whispered, "God, help me." She imagined a soft, warm hug wrapping all around her. Just like that, peace filled her up like a balloon! God's peace is gentle and kind—just like a hug for your heart.

Reflection:

Can you show me how you feel peaceful and calm, knowing God's peace is like a soft hug, just like Mariana?

Today's Prayer:

Dear God, thank you for your gentle peace that feels like a soft hug. Help my heart feel calm and safe, just like Mariana in the garden.

16 DECEMBER

An Invitation to Stillness

Be still and know that I am God.
(Psalm 46:10)

Angelique loves to run and play, but sometimes she sits quietly and listens to the gentle sounds around her. In those still moments, Angelique can feel God's love in her heart. God invites Angelique to be still and remember He is always with her. Every day, Angelique can find peace and comfort by resting quietly with God.

Reflection:

Can you show me how you sit quietly and feel God's love, just like Angelique does in her still moments?

Today's Prayer:

Dear God, thank you for being with me in quiet moments. Help me be still and feel your love and peace in my heart, just like Angelique.

---

17 DECEMBER

The Heart of Generosity

Sharing makes us happy!
(2 Corinthians 9:7)

Sammy loved to gather shiny acorns and play with her friends. One day, she shared her favorite snack with everyone. They giggled, munched, and had so much fun! Sammy's heart felt warm and full. Just like Sammy, when you share with others, your heart shines with joy and love!

Reflection:

Can you show me how you share with others and feel your heart shine with joy, just like Sammy and her friends?

Today's Prayer:

Dear God, thank you for the joy of sharing. Help my heart shine with love and happiness when I give to others, just like Sammy.

18 DECEMBER

God's Perfect Timing

God makes everything beautiful in its time.
(Ecclesiastes 3:11)

Gracie loves to plant seeds and watch them grow into pretty flowers. Sometimes, she wants them to bloom right away, but she learns to wait. God makes everything beautiful at just the right time! When Gracie feels impatient, she can remember that God's timing is perfect. Every day, Gracie can trust God to make her life beautiful, too.

Reflection:

Can you show me how you wait and trust God to make things beautiful, just like Gracie waiting for her flowers to bloom?

Today's Prayer:

Dear God, thank you for making everything beautiful in your time. Help me wait and trust you, just like Gracie with her flowers.

---

19 DECEMBER

Resting in His Goodness

God loves you so much, and you can rest in His kindness! (Psalm 23:6)

Sofie skipped through the sunny meadow, giggling as she played. After a while, she felt sleepy and found a soft, shady spot to rest. As she closed her eyes, she whispered, "God loves me so much." Snuggled up, Sofie felt safe and happy. Just like Sofie, you can rest in God's goodness anytime!

Reflection:

Can you show me how you rest and feel safe, knowing God loves you so much, just like Sofie in the meadow?

Today's Prayer:

Dear God, thank you for loving me so much. Help me rest and feel safe in your kindness, just like Sofie in the meadow.

20
DECEMBER

He Came for You

Jesus loves you so much, little one!
(John 3:16)

Sasha found a soft bunny hopping in the garden. She gently picked it up and gave it a warm hug. "I'll take care of you," she whispered. Just like Sasha loves her bunny, Jesus loves you, little one! Whenever you feel happy or silly, remember, Jesus is smiling at you and loves you always!

Reflection:

Can you show me how you feel loved and cared for, knowing Jesus loves you always, just like Sasha with her bunny?

Today's Prayer:

Dear Jesus, thank you for loving me and caring for me always. Help me feel your love and smile, just like Sasha with her bunny.

21
DECEMBER

Awe and Adoration

God made everything, and He loves you lots!
(Psalm 139:14)

Alina looked at the trees swaying and the flowers dancing in the breeze. The sun was shining, and the sky was so blue! God made all these beautiful things just for you, Alina. When you laugh and play, God smiles because He made you so special. You're part of His wonderful world, and He loves you lots!

Reflection:

When you see the trees moving and the flowers playing in the wind, what makes you smile and feel happy inside?

Today's Prayer:

Dear God, thank you for making the world so beautiful and for loving me so much. Help me smile and feel your love in everything I see.

22
DECEMBER

Grace for the Holidays
God loves us and gives us joy during all times!
(Psalm 30:5)

Eunice watched the little flowers dance, their petals sparkling in the sunshine. "God loves us and brings us joy!" they sang. When snowflakes fell, they softly covered the ground, like a warm hug. Just like the flowers, Eunice's heart was full of joy, knowing God's love is with her all year long.

Reflection:

Can you show me how you feel joyful and loved, knowing God is with you in every season, just like Eunice and the flowers?

Today's Prayer:

Dear God, thank you for loving me and giving me joy in every season. Help my heart feel your love, just like Eunice and the flowers.

23
DECEMBER

Wrapped in His Love
God loves you, little one, just like a warm hug!
(1 John 4:16)

Irene felt a soft breeze one day and imagined it was God's love, wrapping around her like a warm hug. "God loves you, little one," she smiled, feeling cozy and safe. Whether she was playing or resting, Irene knew she was special and loved. God's hugs made her heart smile, and they were always with her.

Reflection:

Can you think of a time when you felt something soft and nice, like a hug? What made you feel cozy and happy, just like God's love?

Today's Prayer:

Dear God, thank you for wrapping me in your love like a warm hug. Help me feel cozy and safe, knowing you are always with me.

24
DECEMBER

A Holy Night
God gave us Jesus, the best gift ever!
(Luke 2:11)

The stars twinkled bright as KC looked up with wide eyes. Long ago, baby Jesus was born, a special gift from God—like the warmest hug or happiest smile! When KC sees the stars, she remembers Jesus shines just for her. Her heart fills with joy, just like that holy night so long ago.

Reflection:

When you look up at the twinkling stars, how do they make you feel inside, just like the special night baby Jesus was born?

———∝———

Today's Prayer:

Dear God, thank you for giving us Jesus, the best gift ever. Help my heart feel joy and wonder every time I see the stars shine.

25
DECEMBER

Joy to the World
Jesus is a special gift to us, bringing love and joy! (Luke 2:11)

Baby Jesus was born in a cozy stable, a special gift from God filled with love and joy! The stars twinkled, and animals gathered close. Mary and Joseph smiled, knowing Jesus would share love with the whole world. Sweet girl, remember—Jesus loves you and He's the happiest gift of all!

Reflection:

Can you show me your biggest smile, knowing Jesus is God's happiest gift, bringing love and joy to you and the whole world?

———∝———

Today's Prayer:

Dear Jesus, thank you for being God's special gift. Fill my heart with your love and joy, and help me share my biggest smile with others.

26
DECEMBER

Peace Beyond the Presents
God gives us peace that makes our hearts happy! (Philippians 4:7)

Luz loved presents, but one day she felt a little sad. Grandma gave her a big hug and said, "God gives us special peace that makes our hearts happy!" Luz closed her eyes and thought of God's love. Her sadness melted away, and her heart sparkled with joy! God's peace is the best gift of all!

Reflection:

Can you show me how you feel happy and peaceful, knowing God's love is the best gift, just like Luz?

Today's Prayer:

Dear God, thank you for your peace that makes my heart happy. Help me remember your love is the best gift, just like Luz.

27
DECEMBER

Looking Back with Gratitude
Thank you, God, for all the happy times! (Psalm 107:1)

Gloria loved playing in the garden with butterflies and colorful flowers. One sunny day, she smiled big and said, "Thank you, God, for all the happy times!" She felt thankful for her toys, her cuddly bear, and fun with friends. Just like Gloria, we can look back and say thank you too!

Reflection:

Can you think of a special time when you played with butterflies or flowers? What made you feel happy and thankful?

Today's Prayer:

Dear God, thank you for all the happy times and special memories. Help me always remember to say thank you, just like Gloria.

28
DECEMBER

Preparing for the New
God makes everything new and special!
(2 Corinthians 5:17)

Donna loved waking up to the sunshine and watching flowers dance in the breeze. "Today feels brand new!" she giggled. When she tried drawing or made a new friend, she knew God was smiling. Just like the flowers, Donna shines bright too—because every day is a new gift from God!

Reflection:

What is something new you would like to try today that will make you smile, just like the flowers dancing in the breeze?

Today's Prayer:

Dear God, thank you for making each day new and special. Help me try new things and shine bright with your love, just like Donna.

29
DECEMBER

He's Already in Tomorrow
God is with us today and tomorrow, so we don't have to worry! (Isaiah 41:10)

Deema loved to play and explore, but sometimes she felt worried about what tomorrow might bring. One day, she heard a gentle voice say, "Deema, don't worry! I'm with you today and tomorrow." It was God! He held her hand, and Deema knew He would always be there, ready for new adventures!

Reflection:

Can you show me how you feel safe and ready for new adventures, knowing God is with you today and tomorrow, just like Deema?

Today's Prayer:

Dear God, thank you for being with me today and tomorrow. Help me feel safe and excited for new adventures, just like Deema.

30 DECEMBER

Finishing the Year in Faith

God loves you every day, and He helps you be brave! (Philippians 1:6)

Ylona loved to swing high in the sky, feeling the breeze and whispering, "God loves me!" His love made her feel brave and strong. As the year came to an end, Ylona remembered how God helped her every day, filling her heart with joy. Just like the swing lifts her high, God's love lifts her heart to finish the year strong in faith!

Reflection:

Can you show me how you feel brave and joyful, knowing God's love helps you finish strong, just like Ylona on her swing?

Today's Prayer:

Thank you, God, for loving me every day and making me brave, like when I swing high. Fill my heart with joy, knowing Your love lifts me up!

---

31 DECEMBER

God's Faithfulness Never Ends

God's love is like a big hug that never goes away! (Psalm 136:1)

Ira loved hugs, and one sunny day, she discovered that God's love is like the biggest hug ever! It's warm, cozy, and never ends. Just like her favorite teddy bear, God's love is always with her, holding her tight. Whenever Ira feels happy or sad, she knows God's love is a forever hug, always there for her!

Reflection:

Can you show me how you feel safe and loved, knowing God's love is a forever hug, just like Ira and her teddy bear?

Today's Prayer:

Dear God, thank you for your love that hugs me forever. Help me feel safe and happy, knowing you are always with me, just like Ira.

What was your favorite part of this book? Let's remember it together!

....
....
....
....
....
....
....
....
....
....
....
....
....
....

I'd love to hear from you...

Your voice holds immeasurable value. if you and your little one found joy in this booK, I would be deeply touched if you could spare a moment to leave a sincere review. Your generous feedbacK is not only greatly appreciated, but it is also incredibly significant.

https://go.binnovatedigital.com/Kidsdevotional

To share your feedbacK, simply scan the QR code with your phone's camera or enter the provided linK into your browser on your phone or computer.

I'm profoundly grateful for your time. ThanK you so much.

Love,
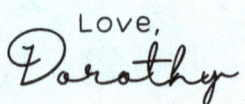

www.ingramcontent.com/pod-product-compliance
Lightning Source LLC
Chambersburg PA
CBHW071733120626
46550CB00002B/508